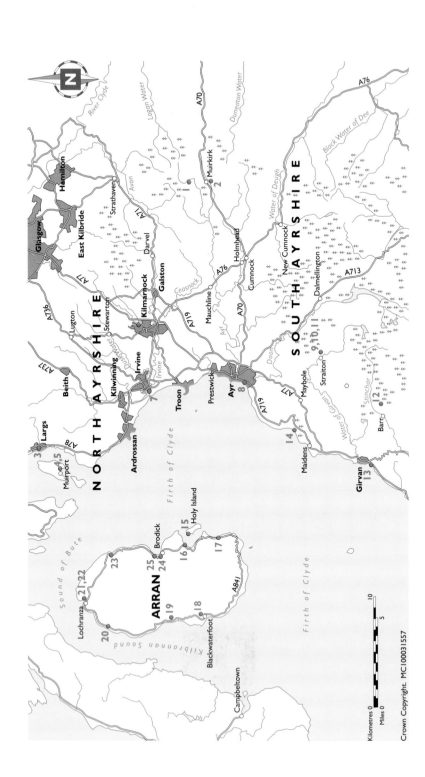

25 WALKS

AYRSHIRE AND ARRAN

Alan Forbes

Series Editor: Roger Smith

mercatpress
www.mercatpress.com

First published 2004
Mercat Press Ltd., 10 Coates Crescent, Edinburgh EH3 7AL
© Mercat Press 2004
ISBN 184183 0348

Acknowledgements

I wish to thank walking consultant David Gray of Ayr for valuable
information given over the 'phone and in the excellent walking leaflets
he has compiled for Barr, Straiton and Girvan. The ScotWays (Scottish
Rights of Way Society) guidebook *Scottish Hill Tracks* also provided
important information for this book. Finally, I wish to thank my good
wife Rosemary for giving me the time off.

Cartography by MapSet Ltd., Newcastle upon Tyne
**Reproduced by permission of Ordnance Survey on behalf of
The Controller of Her Majesty's Stationery Office**
© Crown Copyright 100031557

Printed in Spain by Graficas Santamaría

CONTENTS

USEFUL INFORMATION

The length of each walk is given in kilometres and miles, but within the text, measurements are metric for simplicity. The walks are described in detail and are supported by accompanying maps (study them before you start the walk), so there is little likelihood of getting lost, but if you want a back-up you will find the 1:50,000 Landranger Ordnance Survey maps on sale locally.

Every care has been taken to make the descriptions and maps as accurate as possible, but the author and publishers can accept no responsibility for errors, however caused.

The countryside is always changing and there will inevitably be alterations to some aspects of these walks as times goes by. The publishers and author would be happy to receive comments and suggested alterations for future editions of the book.

METRIC MEASUREMENTS

At the beginning of each walk, the distance is given in miles and kilometres. Within the text, all measurements are metric for simplicity (Ordnance Survey maps are also now all metric). However, a conversion table might be still be useful.

The basic statistic to remember is that one kilometre is five-eighths of a mile. Half a mile is equivalent to 800 metres and a quarter-mile is 400 metres. Below that distance, yards and metres are little different in practical terms.

km	miles
1	0.625
1.6	1
2	1.25
3	1.875
3.2	2
4	2.5
4.8	3
5	3.125
6	3.75
6.4	4
7	4.375
8	5
9	5.625
10	6.25
16	10

Rustic postbox on String Road near Machrie Moor, Arran

INTRODUCTION

Ayrshire and Arran go together like... chalk and cheese?

You can see how neighbouring Argyll and Bute fit nicely together. Yet Ayrshire is so robustly a part of Lowland Scotland and Arran so typically a part of the Highlands and Islands that you might wonder whether a guide-book like this might be at odds with itself.

Arran's attractions need little advertising. After all, the island's Sleeping Warrior profile must be the largest advertising hoarding on the Clyde Coast.

Ayrshire, too, has well-known beauty spots like the River Ayr and Culzean Castle. But it also has deep, haunting areas of moorland whose attractions are less obvious, but with an atmosphere that can seep into the bones.

The John Brown–Bill Shankly walk is one such excursion. It crosses empty grassland where scarcely another walker may be encountered. This walk is one of many being developed in Ayrshire settlements like Muirkirk, Straiton and Barr (the last two must be among the loveliest villages in Scotland). A continuing fascination about so many of the walks in this book is that they go past ordinary communities that produced people who went on to have great destinies.

A sign of the pride Ayrshire and Arran inspire in both visitors and natives is the range and quality of books written about these two distinct areas. Anyone visiting Ayrshire should study *Discovering Ayrshire* by John Strawhorn and Ken Andrew. Grim accounts of the religious killing times are given in Dane Love's *Scottish Covenanting Stories*.

Anyone wanting to learn more about Arran should read Alastair Gemmell's *Discovering Arran* and Robert McLellan's *The Isle of Arran*, which updates Norman Newton's earlier edition. *An Arran Anthology*, edited by Hamish Whyte, takes you on a wonderful literary tour of the island.

There is also a plethora of small local guides. Other books worth reading include Rob Close's *Ayrshire & Arran Architectural Guide*, published by the Royal Incorporation of Architects in Scotland, and two books on stones— Macgregor's *Geology of Arran* published by the Geological Society of Glasgow, and Aubrey Burl's *A Guide to the Stone Circles of Britain, Ireland and Brittany*.

A key point for the walker to note about Ayrshire and Arran is that both areas are extremely accessible. For instance, do not be put off by the ferry crossing to Arran. Transport links are so good that it is possible to leave

Glasgow for Arran in the morning, walk the length of Holy Isle, and be back in Glasgow that evening. Four ferry crossings in one day is not bad going.

The Firth of Clyde, which CalMac's ferry *Caledonian Isles* crosses daily between Ardrossan on the mainland and Brodick on Arran, is a key feature of many walks in this book. These include two on Great Cumbrae, a tiny and delightful island, as well as the beach walk between Irvine and Troon.

Stone, whether rocks formed in geological times, or stood on end in some mysterious pattern by prehistoric man, is another common element of several walks, such as Cock of Arran in the first category, and Machrie Moor in the second.

There are walks to cover all levels of stamina. These include short ones, such as Machrie Moor, and more challenging ones, like the mountain climb to the top of Goatfell. For devotees of Robert Burns, there is an urban walk through Alloway that explores some of the famous landmarks of that great Scot.

To sum up, there is something here for everyone, and I hope you enjoy discovering these walks as much as I have.

ALAN FORBES

TOURIST INFORMATION

For general information on the area covered by this book, accommodation and travel enquiries etc, contact the Ayrshire and Arran Tourist Board, 22 Sandgate, Ayr KA7 1BW, phone 01292 678100, or visit their website at *www.ayrshire-arran.com*.

The main Tourist Information Centre in Ayr is at the address given above and is open all year. There is also a TIC at The Pier, Brodick, on Arran, open all year.

There are seasonal TICs (open from Easter to late October) in Irvine, Largs, Girvan and Millport on Great Cumbrae.

For details of ferry services contact Caledonian MacBrayne on 01475 650100 or at *www.calmac.co.uk*.

The national rail enquiry line is 08457 48 49 50, and timetables can also be found at *www.scotrail.co.uk*.

Opposite: Crew members on ferry *Caledonian Isles* preparing to tie up at Brodick Pier

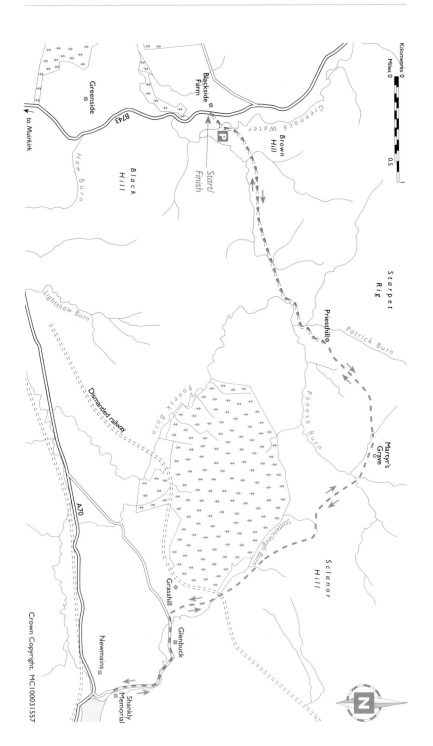

MUIRKIRK HEROES

Bill Shankly and John Brown lived about two miles and three centuries apart, near the Ayrshire village of Muirkirk.

Shankly, the legendary Liverpool manager, coined one of football's most famous aphorisms: 'Some people believe football is a matter of life and death. I am very disappointed with that attitude. I can assure you it is much, much more important than that'. John Brown, a Covenanter, encountered death when he was shot in front of his family by 'Bluidy Clavers'.

This walk leads across high grassy moorland to John Brown's grave. It then continues to the former coalmining village of Glenbuck where Shankly was born, and finally to a memorial erected to 'Shanks'.

About 2km north of Muirkirk, on the A723 road to Strathaven, a signpost stands at a farm road end. The signpost, 'Covenanting Memorial. John Brown', points east towards an apparently empty landscape.

Turn onto the unmetalled farm road. A short distance on, cars can be parked off the road, on the right, just after the entrance to Blackside Farm. Walk along the road towards Priesthill Farm, whose whitewashed walls can be seen on the skyline. As you walk, you will soon discover that this landscape isn't so empty after all.

Apart from the obvious presence of sheep dotted around the hillside, there is the strident 'goback goback' of grouse, the cheerful song of skylark and the plaintive trill of the curlew for company.

INFORMATION

Distance: 15km (9.6 miles) circular.

Start and finish: 2km north of Muirkirk, junction of A723 road to Strathaven and farm road signposted to 'Covenanting Memorial. John Brown'.

Terrain: Water-repellent walking boots or trainers advised. Good, unmetalled road to Priesthill, then track, often faint and boggy over grass moorland. Final stretch down metalled road to Shankly memorial. **Map (Landranger 71) and compass essential for moorland stretch.**

Public Transport: Western Buses services from Ayr, and from Glasgow via Kilmarnock.

Refreshments: Pub and shops in Muirkirk.

Beech trees by a turn in the Ponesk Burn

After a long straight, the road rises above the Ponesk Burn as it swings south towards the River Ayr. On the far bank stands a group of beech trees. The road passes a steading then turns uphill towards Priesthill Farm. Just past the farmhouse, a sign points along a grassy track towards John Brown's grave.

This track, marked by white posts, heads gradually uphill. From the top of the rise, a white gravestone can be seen a short distance ahead. This is John Brown's memorial, the 'Martyr's Grave' shown on the map. Follow the track then turn downhill to cross a stream and reach the memorial, a solitary stone pillar surrounded by a low wall.

John Brown's memorial, a solitary landmark on the moorland

Even by the standards of the 'Killing Times' in late 17th-century Scotland, John Brown's murder was notorious. Ayrshire was a stronghold of the Covenanters, who opposed the imposition of Episcopalianism and bishops. Priesthill was popular for conventicles (clandestine religious gatherings), and Brown's cottage was a meeting place for Covenanters.

Brown was called the 'Christian Carrier' as he took goods around the country on a packhorse. One May morning in 1685, Brown was cutting peat on the moor when he was arrested by dragoons led by John Graham of Claverhouse, a vigorous pursuer of Covenanters. Brown was taken back to his cottage, where he was shot.

The cottage, which stood some 40 metres east of the memorial, has long since disappeared. The memorial was erected with money raised at a service at that spot in 1825.

Rejoin the track, which drops quickly down to a stream before rising uphill again to a sheepfold. At almost 1,300 feet, this is the highest point of the walk. Not high by Cairngorms standards, say, but high enough when bad weather rolls across this exposed landscape.

The track fades through wet, reedy ground before Stottencleugh Burn. Cross the burn then climb a fence beyond the far bank. After more reedy ground, the track reappears and leads through a gap below Sclanor Hill, ahead on the left. Like the sound of your own voice? If so, the wood on your right returns a good echo.

The track goes uphill then along more level ground in the direction of wind turbines on the skyline. Ahead, a barbed-wire fence crosses the route, but the track leads through a gate and downhill to a viaduct on the abandoned Muirkirk–Coalburn railway line. For commercial reasons this never opened.

From the viaduct, continue down to a gate that takes you onto the road beside a steep earth bank that masks an opencast coalmine. A few yards down the road, ruined foundations are all that remain of Glenbuck. Some 50 members of the local Cherrypickers football team turned professional, and several played for Scotland.

Liverpool fans helped preserve Glenbuck's place in football history when they erected a plaque in 1997 to Bill Shankly. The plaque is beside the entrance to Glenbuck Home Farm about 800 metres down the road. Although the road is not busy, there are some blind bends.

The return route can be varied at the viaduct by following the pretty north bank of Stottencleugh Burn for about 300 metres before heading uphill to the gate in the barbed-wire fence.

Steep, grassy banks of Stottencleugh Burn

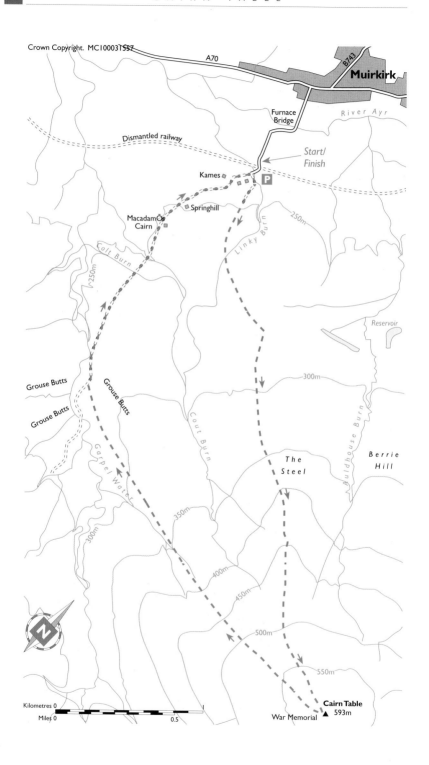

CAIRN TABLE

'**M**uirkirk. Just a Marvellous Place for Walking'. That's the enticing message on the colour leaflet that introduces visitors to walks around this East Ayrshire village. Muirkirk has a remarkable industrial history, but now that industry has gone. The village is reinventing itself as a place where people can enjoy the countryside—and it means business.

A walkers' car park has been established beside the former Kames Institute. Muirkirk Ironworks operated at Kames from 1787 to 1923, but little sign of its buildings remains.

Kames Institute is reached from the main village by a side road that crosses the River Ayr and a dismantled railway. The red sandstone building is easily identified by its clock tower with pointed slate roof. The car park is the starting point for four walks described on a display board that has a leaflet box.

The chief walk is to the summit of Cairn Table, the rounded hill that dominates the southern skyline. Don't be deceived by Cairn Table's benign appearance. Although the ascent involves steady going up a well-defined but at times boggy track, this route is a genuine hill walk.

At 593 metres, or 1,944 feet, the top of Cairn Table can be an inhospitable place for the ill-equipped. Even in the springtime, blizzards can hide the summit, so protective clothing and a knowledge of map and compass are essential.

INFORMATION

Distance: 10.75km (6.75 miles) circular.

Start and finish: Walkers' car park beside Kames Institute, Muirkirk.

Terrain: Map (Landranger 71) and compass essential. Water-resistant footwear needed for very boggy ground on much of the ascent. Stony track on final approach to summit. Descent to old Sanquhar road over even, heather-clad ground. Old road gives comfortable going on return leg to car park.

Public Transport: Western Buses services from Ayr, and from Glasgow via Kilmarnock.

Refreshments: Pub and shops in Muirkirk.

Toilets: In Muirkirk.

Trig point and cairn on summit of Cairn Table

From the car park, walk south on an unmetalled road for about 50 metres then fork left towards a galvanised steel gate. Cross a stile beside a red marker arrow. Continue along the road for a short distance then join a mossy track that leads across a football pitch. This track is marked with white concrete posts and newer wooden waymarkers, with red arrows and a grouse symbol.

If route-finding is no problem, negotiating boggy ground on the lower slopes can be. Much has been done to place wooden boardwalks across streams and stepping stones across bogs. Nevertheless, many small burns run off Cairn Table, so nimble footwork is needed to avoid soggy socks.

Shooting butts in the moorland

About a kilometre on, the track joins a fence and stone dyke that head uphill to the Steel, a point where the track steepens. As the track rises to the Steel, the view opens out across the grouse moor, dotted with sheep, to Muirkirk. North of the village lies more upland country, a rich habitat for birdlife including lapwing, curlew, skylark and hen harrier.

There has been much debate about the Government's decision strictly to enforce European rules to protect the harrier on land that includes the moorland around Muirkirk. Critics say favouring the harrier could harm the bird's prey, including lark and curlew.

The track reaches the summit of Cairn Table—a bouldery plateau distinguished by an Ordnance Survey trig point, a large pyramid cairn and a wonderful view. The cairn was erected in memory of the 87 local men who fell in World War I, and to honour the men and women who returned from that conflict.

A smaller cairn stands a short distance east, just beyond the Ayrshire/Lanarkshire boundary. In clear conditions you can look north to Ben Lomond, west to the island of Arran and south to a brooding sweep of forestry plantations in Dumfries and Galloway. Some 14km west lies Airds Moss. This moor is an important bird habitat and was the scene of a skirmish between Covenanters and dragoons in 1680. The Covenanters were defeated and their leader, Richard Cameron, was among those killed. Cameron's head and hands were cut off and displayed in Edinburgh.

From the top, a track leads onto Cairn Table's western flank before disappearing into the heather. Continue down over good ground to the old road to Sanquhar. On the way you may pass grouse shooting butts dug into the moorland.

Join the road beside the new Sanquhar Brig over Garpel Water and turn right towards Muirkirk. The road soon splits. The left fork leads to Tibbie's Brig, named after a local woman, Tibbie or Isobel Pagan, who is thought to have composed the song *Ca' the Yowes tae the Knowes*.

This road continues to Kames Institute. However, take the right fork that soon passes a cairn. This is a memorial to John Loudon McAdam, the renowned road engineer who was partner in a tarworks where the cairn now stands.

McAdam, born in Ayrshire in 1756, devised a system of improving roads by laying different grades of stone over each other. The system was successfully tested on a stretch of the Muirkirk-Edinburgh road and McAdam later became Britain's chief roads surveyor.

Garpel Water gleaming in the moorland

After the cairn, the road leads through two gates and past a farmhouse, back to the walkers' car park.

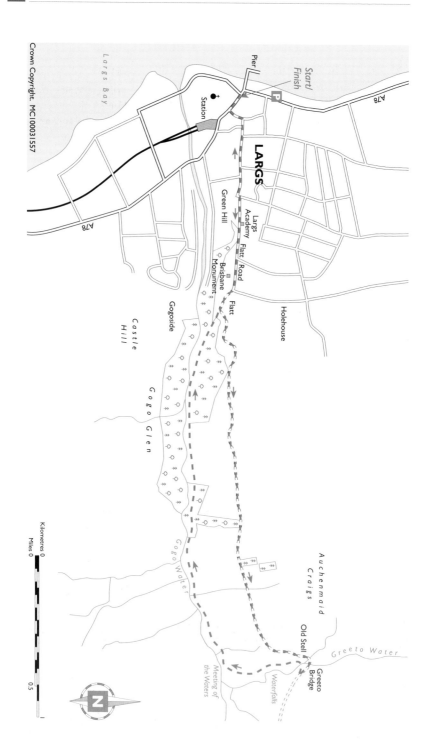

Crown Copyright. MC100031557

GOGO GLEN

Largs is the antithesis of the fading, down-at-heel, British seaside resort. Almost 200 years after wealthy Glaswegians established villas in the town, Largs still attracts thousands of holidaymakers and day trippers. There are the usual attractions including fun fairs and amusement arcades. But these have not smothered Largs' solid character like a cloying candy floss. And Largs boasts the most famous ice cream parlour in Scotland—Nardini's vanilla-white 1930s art deco establishment.

Largs is 'beautifully and salubriously situated' in the Firth of Clyde. The town nestles at the foot of the North Ayrshire hills and looks a short distance over to the island of Great Cumbrae. This walk takes full advantage of Largs' position by offering an easy climb to a vantage point overlooking the town and the Firth. It finishes with a pleasant woodland stroll back down to the town.

From the Great Cumbrae ferry pier, walk along Main Street, turn left into Bellman's Close then right into Gateside Street. Cross over at a junction and walk along Flatt Road, passing Largs Academy.

INFORMATION

Distance: 6.75km (4.2miles) circular.

Start and finish: Great Cumbrae ferry pier.

Terrain: Pavements and unmetalled road to Greeto Bridge. Sometimes boggy track and woodland path through Gogo Glen.

Public Transport: Frequent train service from Glasgow Central Station to Largs.

Refreshments: Large choice of cafes and pubs in Largs.

Toilets: In Largs.

Opening Hours: *Vikingar Centre*: Mon, Wed, Fri 10.00-22.00; Tue, Thurs 09.00-22.00; Sat, Sun 10.00-16.00. Telephone (01475) 689777 for *Viking Experience* times.

Great Cumbrae ferry arriving at Largs

Turn right into Bellsdale Avenue, then turn left to join an unmetalled road leading uphill to a gate, with a sign requesting visitors to keep dogs on a lead, because sheep graze on the grassy hillside.

The road, now metalled, twists and turns up through woodland then comes out into the open beside sheepfolds on the left. Continue for a few metres to a gate then cross a fence by a stile. The road, from now on more a broad, unmetalled track, gradually climbs the side of the hill. Down to your right you may hear the sound of water tumbling through the famous beauty spot of Gogo Glen. Looking back to Largs, the walk keeps its promise with a beautiful view to Great Cumbrae and, a short distance further west, the island of Bute.

Out of sight, on the southern edge of the town, stands the Pencil monument. This commemorates a vital moment in Scottish history. In 1263 King Haakon IV of Norway sent a fleet to assert his influence over the west of Scotland. Haakon's fleet was badly damaged by a storm as it lay anchored beside the Cumbraes. His warriors were beaten near Largs in a battle with the army of the Scottish king, Alexander III. This episode marked the end of the era of Viking conquest. The town's Vikingar visitor centre tells the saga of the Vikings in Scotland. In late summer a Viking festival features a re-enactment of the battle, a longship burning and a torchlit procession.

Continue for a short distance to another gate where the fence is crossed by a stile. Pass a plantation on the right that stretches down to Gogo Glen.

Shortly after the trees, the gradient eases. The track swings left, hugging the hillside, then arrives at Greeto Bridge. Here, a wooden bridge replaces the old stone arch that vaulted over Greeto Water. Greeto Bridge is a lovely spot for a picnic. Greeto Water, above and below the bridge, contains pools of dark brown water.

Bridge over Greeto Water

From the bridge, follow a narrow path downhill beside the west bank of Greeto Water.

A short distance below the bridge, you will have to make an easy clamber over a low rock shelf. The path continues downhill past a series of pools and small cascades to the meeting with Gogo Water.

The path descends Gogo Glen, which is very pretty but boggy in places. Go through a hole in a fence to enter the plantation mentioned earlier. A couple of trees lying over the path provide agility tests. The walk continues past rock shelves and pools. Along this way, boulders and tree roots have to be crossed. This is a stretch that young children will enjoy if they are taken by the hand.

The path eventually opens out into a broad woodland path, firm and comfortable underfoot. Pass a footbridge on the left, then, about 200 metres on, take the right fork to leave the woodland and rejoin Bellsdale Avenue.

A short distance west of Bellsdale Avenue is a small mound called Green Hill. Here stand three pillars that were used for astronomy by Sir Thomas Brisbane, one-time governor of New South Wales in Australia, who was born in Largs. By the time of his death in 1860, Sir Thomas had catalogued more than 7,000 stars.

After examining the pillars, return to the sea front for a well-deserved ice cream.

Nardini's ice cream parlour, Largs

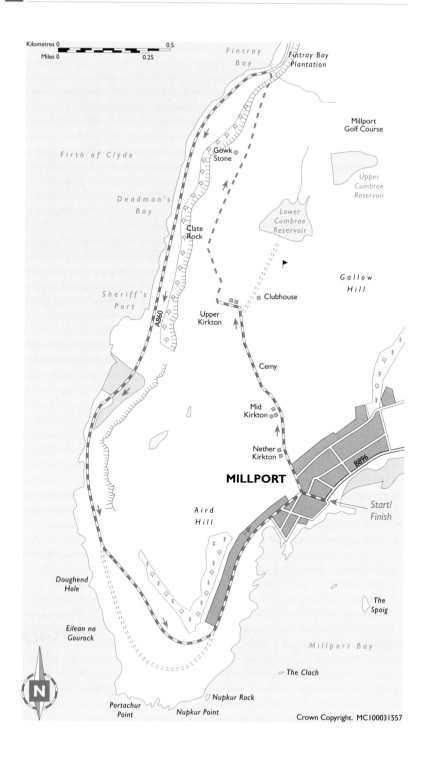

Kilometres 0   0.5
Miles 0   0.25

Fintray Bay

Fintray Bay Plantation

Millport Golf Course

Firth of Clyde

Gowk Stone

Upper Cumbrae Reservoir

Deadman's Bay

Lower Cumbrae Reservoir

Clate Rock

Gallow Hill

Sheriff's Port

Clubhouse

A860

Upper Kirkton

Cemy

Mid Kirkton

Nether Kirkton

MILLPORT

B896

Start/ Finish

Aird Hill

Doughend Hole

The Spoig

Eilean na Gourock

Millport Bay

The Clach

Nupkur Rock

Portachur Point   Nupkur Point

Crown Copyright. MC100031557

N

GREAT CUMBRAE TO FINTRAY BAY

W hat's so great about Great Cumbrae? On the face of it, nothing much. The island measures less than 6km from top to bottom and the adjective 'Great' serves simply to distinguish Great Cumbrae from its even more diminutive neighbour, Little Cumbrae.

Once on the island, however, bald statistics cease to matter. Strange things happen: time seems to slow down, people cycle on the wrong side of the road, and scientists fall prey to romanticism.

The scientists in question belong to Johns Hopkins University in the USA. Describing courses at the island's University Marine Biological Station, Johns Hopkins talks of Great Cumbrae's 'mountains' and its 'downtown' area. Now Millport is no Manhattan and the island's tallest summit is pasture at an altitude of 120 or so metres, but the American visitors have still managed to capture the charm of Great Cumbrae.

They describe 'a breathtaking contrast of beaches and forests and fields... countless opportunities for biking, walking and hiking'. Not to mention sailing, as the island is home to Scotland's National Water Sports Centre.

All this seems a world away from the buzz of Glasgow city centre. Yet the frequent train service from Glasgow's Central Station to Largs on the Ayrshire coast takes little more than an hour. From Largs, the ferry crossing to Great Cumbrae lasts only 10 minutes. Waiting at Cumbrae Slip are shuttle buses that take visitors the short distance to Cumbrae's one main settlement, the town of Millport.

Still, clear water in Millport harbour

It is easy to see why generations of people from the Glasgow area chose to come 'doon the watter' to Millport for their holidays. The small town stretches round its sheltered bay that faces south to Little Cumbrae. Most of the two- and three-storey buildings on the front are white-washed. The harbour at the west end of the town has room for yachts and a sandy beach just big enough to delight children with buckets and spades.

This walk heads north to Fintray Bay, roughly half-way up the west coast of Great Cumbrae. Along the way are outstanding views of the Firth of Clyde.

The walk starts at the old pier beside the harbour in Millport. Walk along Cardiff Street then turn right onto Golf Road, passing a bowling club on the right. Golf Road runs uphill from the town passing Nether and Mid Kirkton farms, a small cemetery and a holiday caravan park.

Golf Road ends, fittingly, at Millport Golf Course. A right fork leads to the clubhouse. Instead take the left fork to Upper Kirkton Farm which has riding stables.

Just before the gate into the courtyard, turn left along a narrow track then pass through a kissing gate into a field. Turn right and follow a track heading north beside a fence. Soon, the fence swings off to the right. Leaving the fence behind, follow the track across fields overlooking the Firth of Clyde.

The view from the track is outstanding. Directly opposite, barely 5km across the water, lies Kilchattan Bay on the island of Bute. To the south-west is the island of Arran, dominated by Goatfell and its neighbouring mountains. Northwards, the high chimney of Inverkip power station can be seen, about 11km up the Ayrshire coast.

After passing through two open gates on the way through the fields, the track approaches a landmark a short distance down to the left. This wedge-shaped boulder pushing out of the turf is the Gowk Stone. This is one of several gowk (the Scots word for cuckoo) stones around the country. Great Cumbrae is particularly rich in bird life, and birdsong provides a pleasant accompaniment on the walk.

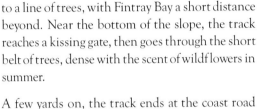

The Gowk Stone

After the Gowk Stone, the track drops downhill to a line of trees, with Fintray Bay a short distance beyond. Near the bottom of the slope, the track reaches a kissing gate, then goes through the short belt of trees, dense with the scent of wildflowers in summer.

A few yards on, the track ends at the coast road around the island. Turn right to visit Fintray Bay, a popular spot for visitors, or turn left for Millport.

The way back to town involves a pleasant walk along a pavement littered with empty seashells left by predatory oyster catchers. Birdsong is often drowned out by excited cyclists who have hired bikes at Millport for the popular 15km round-island ride. Cars pass so infrequently on Great Cumbrae that absent-minded cyclists often drift across the road.

A few yards inland, seabirds including kittiwake and fulmar nest on cliffs, while in the opposite direction, seals may be seen, sticking their snouts out of the sea. To the south, Little Cumbrae, with its cliffs and lighthouse dating from 1755, draws attention until the coast road swings north to enter Millport for the end of the walk and the bus back to the ferry.

Rocky shoreline on the way back to Millport

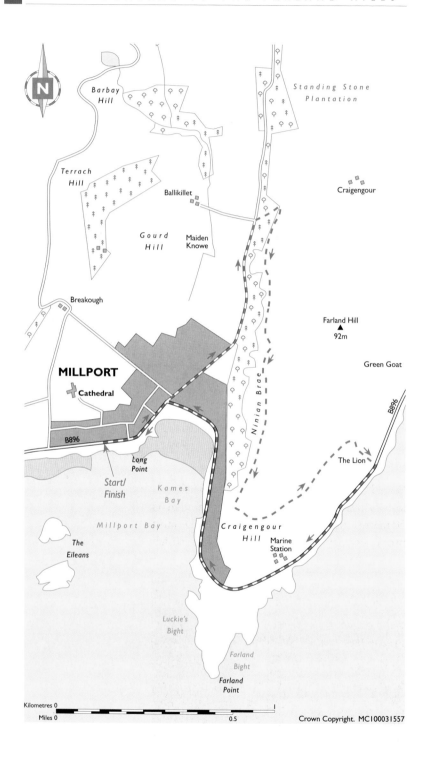

Crown Copyright. MC100031557

GREAT CUMBRAE TO THE FARLAND HILLS

On a fine day the 10-minute ferry ride from Largs to Great Cumbrae gives no cause for foreboding. As the island draws nearer, passengers gaze expectantly at the landscape—a refreshing variety of greens formed by bracken and woodland on grassy hillsides where sheep may safely graze.

No wonder, then, that visitors in the shuttle bus to Millport are startled when they turn a corner and see an enormous iguana crawling up a grassy bank. This, of course, is no real lizard, but a fantastically shaped lump of rock. A rock, however, that could give a drunk person a nasty fright on a dark night.

From further up the hill the iguana becomes, in many eyes, a lion. And it is as the Lion Rock that this landmark has come to be known.

The Lion Rock is one of several huge trap dikes on Great Cumbrae. These are the result of molten hard rock forcing its way up between red sandstone which gradually becomes worn away.

Fears have been raised that the Lion Rock may lose its 'head', because a crack has appeared in its 50-metre-long form. The Lion Rock is the most prominent physical feature on this walk, which

Classic view of Millport from Farland Hills

starts beside Kames Bay at the east end of Millport and then crosses the attractive Farland Hills overlooking the town.

From Glasgow Road, which faces the bay, walk east along Kelburn Street, then continue out of town along Ferry Road. Beyond the last houses, keep to the pavement along the pleasant country road that eventually joins the coast road. The pavement is flanked by a stone wall at the base of the wooded slopes of the Farland Hills.

About 1 km from town you arrive opposite the entrance to Ballikillet Farm. Here, climb stone steps set into the wall and follow a track up through the wood. At the top of the wood, climb a stile to enter a field. Turn right and follow a fence round the edge of the wood, passing a small wooden cabin on the way.

Beyond the cabin, you reach a fence running downhill. Cross this fence by wooden rails where it joins the fence you have been following. Follow the first fence, alongside the wood, then join a farm track that leads further along the eastern flank of the Farland Hills. It is on this side of the hills that a classic view of Millport opens up.

Continue through gorse and rough pasture to a red sandstone cairn for the best view of the town. The seafront, the harbour and yachts in the bay are framed by trees lower down the hillside. In the town, the spire of the Cathedral of the Isles, believed to be Europe's smallest cathedral, rises over the rooftops.

Coast road and Hunterston Bulk Terminal, through a window in Lion Rock

Turn round and the next thing you see are the tops of two large cranes peering over the brow of the Farland Hills. Walk towards these cranes along a track that leads over the brow. On the other side, the cranes can be seen on a jetty at the Hunterston Bulk Terminal, some 2km away on the mainland.

The Hunterston peninsula has been a place of broken dreams for Scottish industry. Its flat land and deep water promised much, but the terminal was intended to supply iron ore for a withering steel industry and the adjacent oil construction yard never met its full potential. Just to the south sits the Hunterston B nuclear power station, due to close around 2011.

The sea around here has long been the key to power and prosperity. It is believed that in 1263 King Haakon IV of Norway was standing a short distance north of the Farland Hills when he saw his fleet damaged by a storm. Haakon's ensuing defeat at the Battle of Largs marked an end to Norse influence in Scotland.

The only disturbance now, as you continue along the track, seems to come from jet skiers as they scud through the Fairlie Roads between Great Cumbrae and the mainland.

Soon the track arrives at a low stone dyke that runs downhill to merge with the Lion Rock. Cross the dyke, then head down to admire the rock and join the coast road. Turn right to walk back towards Millport. A few hundred metres further takes you past the island's University Marine Biological Station, with its museum and aquarium open to the public.

Continue into Millport, or walk a short distance further to a bus shelter where you can wait for the shuttle bus to take you back to Cumbrae Slip and the ferry for Largs.

Lion Rock lumbers up the hillside

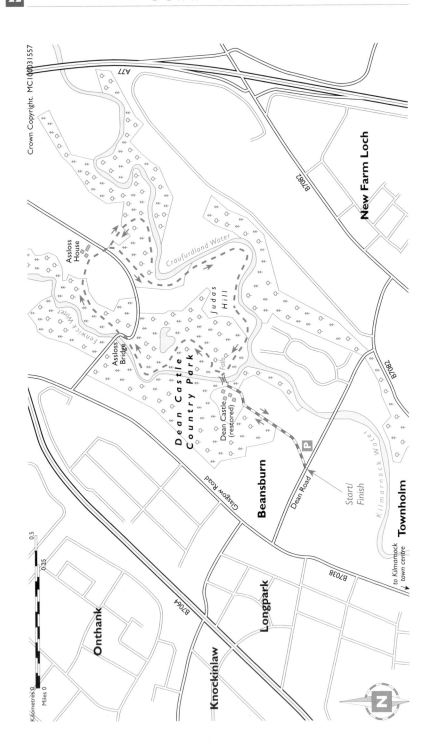

Crown Copyright. MCI 00031557

DEAN CASTLE

The children of Kilmarnock must be a happy breed to have a place like Dean Castle Country Park on their doorstep. Any youngster fascinated by knights of old or blood and thunder should find that the castle and its woodland provide a feast for the imagination.

Visitors approaching the castle by the main driveway will be impressed by the tall, square keep to the left. This forbidding tower was built in the 14th century by the powerful Boyd family, who received their lands at Kilmarnock from Robert the Bruce. To the right is a later addition, the more luxurious palace range.

Dean Castle offers a wonderful day out. The main tower contains a grand hall with minstrels' gallery and a dungeon reached by a ladder. Views of the surrounding countryside can be had from wooden walkways round the battlements. These were constructed by the 8th Lord Howard de Walden, who carried out a sympathetic restoration of the castle in the early 20th century. His successor, the 9th Earl, gifted the castle and grounds to the people of Kilmarnock.

The castle's outstanding collections of arms and armour, tapestries and early musical instruments, including lutes and spinets, are themselves worth a visit. Many visitors, however, come to sample the attractions that lie outside the castle. Dean Castle Country Park lies north of Kilmarnock town centre. The entrance is on Dean Road which runs off Glasgow Road.

From the entrance a road leads past the car park towards the castle. Follow this road, passing the visitor centre to the left and the large grassy area in front of the castle that is popular with picnicking families.

INFORMATION

Distance: 3.5km (2.2 miles) circular.

Start and finish: Entrance to Dean Castle Country Park.

Terrain: Well surfaced paths.

Public transport: The park is 1.5km (one mile) north of bus and rail stations in Kilmarnock town centre.

Refreshments: Tearoom at country park. Wide variety in Kilmarnock.

Toilets: At three locations in the park.

Opening hours: The Country Park and Visitor Centre are open all year. Dean Castle is open Apr-Oct daily 1200-1700, Nov-Mar Sat-Sun 1200-1600. Admission free. Enquiries: 01563 522702. Website: *www.deancastle.com*

Dean Castle

Follow the road round the right-hand side of the castle and over the bridge above Fenwick Water. This attractive tree-lined river flows over rock shelves and has boulders piled up on either bank.

Follow signs for the children's corner. At this popular family attraction, peacocks strut around and children can view ducks, geese and small birds including canaries. At the far end is an intriguing metal dragon. A path leads out of the children's corner and passes a large pond where you may see swans. Turn right onto a path that follows the Fenwick Water.

The path, well surfaced with gravel, passes a wetland pond full of water plantlife. A short distance on, pass a car park beside the old stone bridge on Assloss Road, the tarmac access road through part of the country park.

Clydesdale horse led through woods

Just beyond the car park, believed to have been the site of a stone quarry, join a path (signed 'No Cycling') that enters the wood and rises up above the river. Soon, conifers are replaced by broadleaved trees as the path heads towards the park's riding centre. You may see squirrels in the trees here. Beyond the centre, cross Assloss Road and follow a track straight ahead, downhill past a ruined cottage to a walled garden.

The track swings right, round the side of the garden, and continues to a footbridge that crosses Craufurdland Water. Just before the bridge, a path leads down to the water where supervised children might enjoy exploring the riverbank.

Retrace your steps past the walled garden and cottage towards Assloss Road. A few metres before the road, turn left into a path that goes through woods above Craufurdland Water. This path drops down towards the river, passing a field where you may see red deer, and then paddocks for rare sheep. This river was diverted to its present course in the early 1800s, possibly to correspond with estate and farm boundaries.

The path now follows Craufurdland Water, whose banks are a magnet for young explorers. The river makes a big swing to the right and, about 600 metres further on, the Craufurdland and Fenwick join to become Kilmarnock Water, which eventually joins the River Irvine on the southern edge of Kilmarnock.

Kilmarnock Water once powered a bonnet-makers' factory nearby. Bonnet making became an incorporated trade in 1647 and was for many years the town's main industry. The broad, flat Kilmarnock bonnets or 'cowls' were commonly worn in the Scottish Lowlands. Another popular piece of Kilmarnock headgear was the red and blue striped nightcap. One 19th-century writer facetiously commented: 'Those nightcaps still figure grotesquely on venerable or hoary heads, and have often provoked the flash of wit and the scathing of satire'.

The path swings away from the river and passes through a cutting to bring you back to the bridge near the castle. It would be premature to cross the bridge and head for home. Instead, turn right and follow signs to the rare breeds centre a short distance away, near the children's corner. Woolly rarities include Portland, Hebridean and North Ronaldsay sheep and pygmy goats.

Hebridean sheep

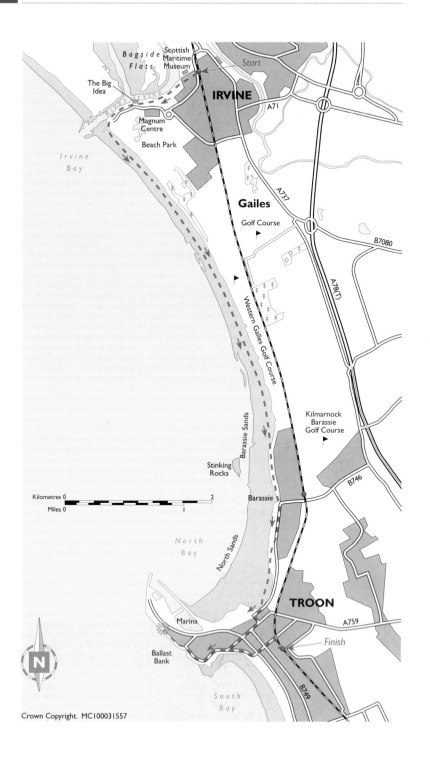

IRVINE TO TROON BEACH WALK

The Ayrshire coast has long been a magnet for pleasure seekers. Its waters have provided sport for sailors, now joined by wind surfers and jet skiers. Many a sandcastle has been built on its long, sandy beaches, and proud reputations won and lost on its famous links golf courses. This walk follows the curve of the beautiful beach that runs south from the bustling New Town of Irvine to the more sedate golfing resort of Troon.

Irvine is an ancient Royal Burgh on the Ayrshire coast that became a new town in 1966. This mixing of old with new works well, particularly at the town's Harbourside, where old terraced cottages rub shoulders with modern houses that echo but do not ape their elders.

Much of the town's prosperity was based on the River Irvine, which provided safe anchorage for cargo boats. For several centuries, many of the goods bound to and from Glasgow passed through Irvine.

The walk begins at Harbourside, home to the Scottish Maritime Museum and the Magnum Leisure Centre. On the north side of the harbour entrance stands the now defunct Big Idea. This dramatic building was a museum that celebrated inventions and inventors. Sadly, it closed in 2003 because it failed to attract enough visitors to remain viable.

INFORMATION

Distance: 11.5km (7.2 miles) linear.

Start: Harbourside, Irvine.

Finish: Troon Railway Station. Return by train.

Terrain: Sandy beach, pavement walking in Irvine and Troon, scramble over low boulders to leave beach at Troon.

Public transport: Regular train service from Glasgow Central Station to Irvine and Troon.

Refreshments: Wide choice at Irvine and Troon.

Toilets: In Irvine, Barassie and Troon.

Opening hours: *Scottish Maritime Museum:* 10.00-17.00 (summer); 10.00-16.00 (winter).

To start the walk, follow signs through the town for Harbourside, then head for the nearby Beach Park. Train travellers arriving at Irvine Railway Station should walk under the bridge marked 'Harbourside' and walk along Montgomery

Sandstone dragon overlooking Irvine beach

Street and Harbour Street. A good landmark to spot near the mouth of the Irvine is the tall square tower that was the automatic tide marker station for the harbour. From here it is just a matter of a few yards to the beach, and a first sight of Troon in the distance.

On the beach, your feet crunch through a gritty mix of crushed shells. Keep a sharp eye out as you walk along the shore, for there be dragons lurking above in the long grass—well, at least a red sandstone dragon hatched by the old Irvine New Town Corporation. This dragon, its scaly tail wrapped round itself, is one of several pieces of civic art created for the new town, and it gives enormous pleasure to children who clamber over its friendly form.

A noticeboard on a neighbouring hillock describes the local wildlife, including terns and cormorants, and explains how this area, once covered in industrial waste, was reclaimed. As you continue along the beach, the sounds of ardent conversations may drift over the dunes that rise up from the beach. Climb the dunes and you will see that these voices come from any one of a string of golf courses that line this route—Gailes, Western Gailes, Barassie and Royal Troon.

Stinking Rocks, with Ailsa Troon shipyard in the distance

Reminding yourself that golf is just a good walk spoiled, return to the beach and enjoy the seascape to your right. Out to sea sits the Island of Arran, with Goatfell and its neighbouring hills forming the outline likened to a sleeping warrior. South of Arran is the rounded volcanic plug of Ailsa Craig. Just offshore to the south of Troon is Lady Isle with its lighthouse; its position relative to Ailsa Craig is a good indicator of progress along the beach.

At Barassie, on the outskirts of Troon, the oddly named Stinking Rocks lie scattered on the shore. Here, supervised children can scramble on the mussel-encrusted outcrop and explore its rock pools.

As you pass the houses on the Barassie seafront, the large shed at Ailsa Troon shipyard looms larger. Closer to Troon, large pools and streams may have to be splashed through, or jumped across if you prefer.

Finally at Troon, with its solid stone houses, you are forced to quit the beach just before the Pan Rocks promontory. Scramble over low boulders laid down to prevent sea erosion and turn right onto North Shore Road. At the end of this road, turn left down Barassie Street, then right along Portland Street and West Portland Street. Next, turn right onto St Clair Terrace, facing South Bay. Continue along Portland Terrace and Titchfield Road to a high embankment. This is the Ballast Bank, constructed of rubble brought by boats that had taken coal to Ireland. Construction of the bank was ordered by the Duke of Portland, who in the 19th Century turned Troon into one of Scotland's busiest ports. A summit viewfinder points out landmarks around a 360° panorama.

Retrace your steps along Titchfield Road, continue along to the South Beach Esplanade then turn left down St Meddan's Street to Troon Railway Station. Frequent train services take you back to Irvine.

View from the Ballast Bank

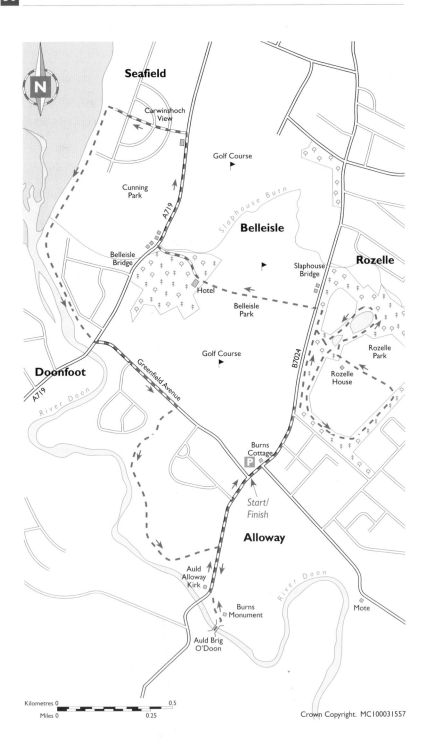

Seafield

Carwinshoch View

Golf Course

Cunning Park

A719

Slaphouse Burn

Belleisle

Belleisle Bridge

Rozelle

Slaphouse Bridge

Hotel

Belleisle Park

Golf Course

Doonfoot

Greenfield Avenue

A719

River Doon

B7024

Rozelle Park

Rozelle House

Burns Cottage

P

Start/ Finish

Alloway

River Doon

Auld Alloway Kirk

Burns Monument

Mote

Auld Brig O'Doon

Kilometres 0   0.5
Miles 0   0.25

Crown Copyright. MC100031557

ROBERT BURNS' ALLOWAY

Many would argue that Ayrshire's most famous son was the greatest Scot who ever lived.

Robert Burns had what is now termed a complicated personal life. He may not have been a valiant warrior like Wallace or Bruce. But his poetry has for over 200 years been an inspiration to people around the world who value basic human dignity and freedom. Or, as Burns wrote: 'The rank is but the guinea's stamp/ The man's the gowd for a' that'.

This walk goes through Alloway, on the southern edge of Ayr, where Burns was born.

Start at Burns Cottage car park, at the corner of Greenfield Avenue and Monument Road. Turn left onto Monument Road and walk 100 metres to the cottage.

It was in this small house, with clay walls, thatched roof and tiny windows, that Robert Burns was born in the winter of 1759. Burns' father, William, built the house and helped lay the foundation for his oldest son's success by finding him the best available education. Burns' mother, Agnes, could not write, but she and a friend, Betty Davidson, 'cultivated the latent seeds of poesy' with folk tales told round the fireside. The cottage and adjacent museum tell Burns' life story using memorabilia and audiovisual displays.

INFORMATION

Distance: 8.5km (5.2 miles) circular.

Start and finish: Burns Cottage car park, Monument Road, Alloway.

Terrain: Pavements, woodland path and short shore walk.

Public transport: Western Buses services to and from Ayr Bus Station. Frequent trains to Ayr from Glasgow.

Refreshments: Tea room in Rozelle House, restaurant in Tam o'Shanter Experience. Wide choice in Ayr.

Toilets: Ayr Station, Rozelle House, Belleisle Park, Esplanade.

Opening hours: *Burns National Heritage Park*: 09.30-17.30 (April-Oct); 10.00-17.00 (Nov-Mar). *Rozelle House*: 10.00-17.00, Sun 14.00-17.00 (April-Oct). Closed Sun Oct-Mar.

Burns Cottage

Continue north along Monument Road for about 500 metres and cross over to enter Rozelle Estate. Pass the lodge and turn right to join a woodland nature trail round the estate featuring a wide variety of trees including Douglas fir and monkey puzzle (Chilean pine). Halfway round the trail, join a tarmac road that leads back to the estate entrance, passing Rozelle House. This building houses South Ayrshire Council's museum and art collection, and a special attraction are the exuberant paintings of Alexander Goudie that depict old Ayrshire and scenes from Burns' famous epic poem *Tam o' Shanter*. Before leaving the estate, turn right before the lodge to visit two picturesque ponds, haunt of swans and mallard ducks.

Back at the estate entrance, cross Monument Road, turn right and walk about 50 metres to the entrance of Belleisle Park. Enter the park and follow a surfaced path between two golf courses, Belleisle and Seafield. The path leads to Belleisle House, a hotel and restaurant which also holds the golf clubhouse. Turn right before the building, take the path on the left at the toilets, cross the car park and follow the driveway onto Racecourse Road.

Cross Racecourse Road, turn right, and in about 500 metres turn left into Carwinshoch View, which leads to the Esplanade beside a sandy beach. Head south along the Esplanade to cross Slaphouse Burn and reach the mouth of the River Doon. Further down the coast, Greenan Castle, once a stronghold of the powerful Kennedy family, crumbles on the Heads of Ayr, a volcanic cliff that plunges more than 60m to the sea.

Auld Brig o' Doon

Pass a beach shelter and join a path along the north bank of the River Doon. You might hear the 'whop, whop, flappa, flappa' of a swan flying down the river and landing on the water. This pretty riverside stretch, rich in wild flowers, is flanked on the left by a beech hedge almost bent double by the wind.

The path ends at Doonfoot Road, a continuation

of Racecourse Road. Cross over and continue up Greenfield Avenue for about 600 metres, then turn right through an entrance in a wall marked with South Ayrshire Council signs. Walk about 300 metres along an unmetalled road, then take a right fork downhill towards the River Doon.

Here, the woodland and fast-flowing river inspired Robert Burns to write 'Ye banks and braes o' bonnie Doon/ How can ye bloom sae fresh and fair?' The path ends at steps leading up to Shanter Way, which in turn joins Monument Road.

Turn right to reach Alloway's Old Kirk, the setting for the demon revelry in *Tam o' Shanter*. In the poem, Tam, riding back from the alehouse, disturbs Satan's celebrations and is pursued by witches. Luckily his grey mare Meg carries him over Auld Brig o' Doon to safety, as witches cannot cross running water. Meg, however, loses her tail to a witch who has grabbed hold of it.

The roofless Old Kirk, in whose churchyard Burns' father is buried, still evokes an eerie atmosphere. Across the road is the Tam o'Shanter Experience, a visitor attraction with an audiovisual presentation of Tam's frightening journey.

From the Kirk, cross Monument Road, turn right and walk a short distance downhill to the steeply arched Brig o' Doon where Tam escaped the witches. On the way you pass the Grecian-style Burns Monument.

The bridge gives an excellent view of a particularly pretty part of the river. Return to the car park, 500 metres north along Monument Road.

Alloway's Old Kirk

Crown Copyright. MC100031557

THE STRAITON TO PATNA HILL TRACK

I n earlier generations, most people had only one method of visiting their neighbours—on foot.

The countryside was criss-crossed by a network of paths between communities. In many places, the dead even had to be carried long distances to the nearest graveyard along often mountainous 'coffin roads'.

Many of these paths have disappeared and are forgotten. Some remain only as lines on maps. This route forms part of a hill track between Straiton and Patna. Although the route's appearance bears little relationship to what it would have looked like originally, it does provide an extremely interesting excursion.

This walk begins at Straiton, and unless transport is waiting at Patna, the return journey involves some 16km of walking over often rough and boggy ground. From the centre of Straiton, walk north along the B741 Dalmellington road for about 500m until you reach a tarmac road turning left over Lambdoughty Burn. Beside the entrance a waymarker with a yellow arrow indicates the Straiton-Patna Hill Track.

A short distance on, a sign points to Sclenteuch Moor, further along the route. The tarmac road leads past Sclenteuch Farm on the right, then steepens to give a fine view to Straiton and the surrounding hills and woodland.

INFORMATION

Distance: 16km (10 miles) circular.

Start and finish: Walkers' car park, Straiton.

Terrain: Short stretch of tarmac road followed by forestry roads and tracks. Boggy in places, especially after rain. Map and compass recommended.

Public transport: Western Buses services to and from Ayr.

Refreshments: Inn at Straiton.

Toilets: In Straiton.

Patna War Memorial overlooking Doon Valley

The road enters a forestry plantation. Ignore a ladder stile over a dry stone dyke on the left. The stile is on the route of the local Hill Wood walk. Continue along the road which narrows to a track. A couple of small streams cross the track and the ground can be muddy.

Cross a forestry road, following a post with a white arrow. The track now takes a deep-cut way through the peat of Sclenteuch Moor. Ignore a second forestry road branching left and continue towards tall Scots pines beside the ruins of Dhu Loch cottage, marked as a sheepfold on the map. To the north you can glimpse Loch Spallander reservoir.

Loch Spallander

The next stage of the route leads to the small burn that runs into Loch Spallander. For most of the way the track heads north-east by forestry rides marked with white arrow signposts. The track then swings north, crosses a forestry road and runs downhill through a ride to the small wooden bridge over the burn.

Cross the bridge, turn left and follow a track about 200 metres to Loch Spallander. At the loch's reedy edge cross another small bridge to regain the south side of the burn. For a better view of the loch and its swans, follow a track that skirts the trees on the south shore. Loch Spallander is a genuine unspoilt beauty spot, frequented only by anglers and walkers.

Return to the first bridge then turn left uphill, following a stone dyke. At the top of this slope, a line of electricity pylons crosses the route. These pylons form part of the Scotland-Ireland electricity interconnector. This £200 million Scottish Power project to provide electricity to Northern Ireland was strongly opposed in the south-west of Scotland as communities feared the pylons would spoil local scenery.

At the time of writing, this scheme had made its own mark on the Straiton–Patna Hill Track. Vehicles used for tree felling and pylon erection had churned up several hundred metres of track. The section of dyke where the pylons cross the route had become a pile of boulders. Scottish Power gave the assurance, however, that the track would be made good and drainage installed.

Just before the pylons, go through a gap in the dyke then continue uphill with the dyke on your right. Pass old stone sheep pens then go through a gap in the dyke. Head north downhill on tussocky ground to a forestry road.

Following the dyke beside the hill path

You can turn right and follow this road. A more interesting way is to cross the road and continue downhill with the dyke still to your left.

At the bottom of the hill, join a broad forestry ride that swings uphill to your right. The top of this ride joins the last forestry road you crossed. Turn left and follow the road through Patna forest, ignoring branch roads. The forestry road ends at a minor road some 200 metres from the Patna boundary. A good finishing point is the village's war memorial, perched on a grassy knoll. The climb to the memorial is rewarded with an outstanding view over the Doon Valley.

This area was famous for collieries and blast furnaces. These industries are dead, but their memory lives on at the Dunaskin Heritage Centre, at a former ironworks in Waterside, and the Scottish Industrial Railway Centre in Dalmellington—one of Scotland's official Book Towns.

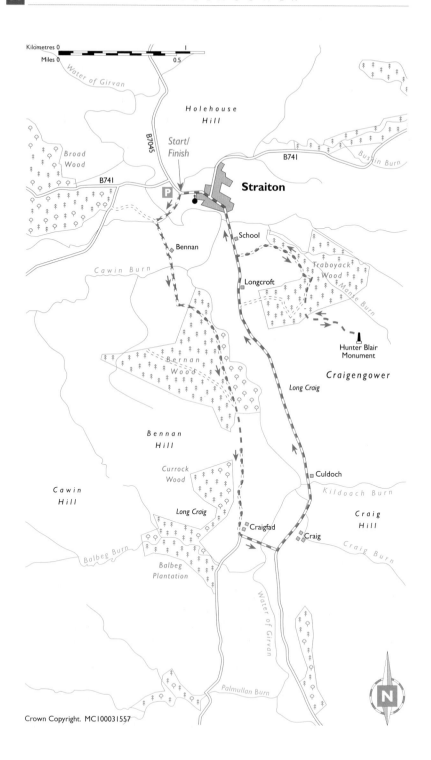

Crown Copyright. MC100031557

CRAIGENGOWER

Straiton is widely considered to be Ayrshire's prettiest village. Indeed Maurice Lindsay, the distinguished writer and former director of the Scottish Civic Trust, believes it is one of the most attractive villages in Scotland. Straiton sits among rich farmland and forest, with Maybole to the west and Dalmellington to the east. Much of the main street, with its facing rows of picturesque cottages, straddles an unclassified road that leads south to the wilder bounds of the Carrick Forest.

Straiton's lovely setting, beside the Water of Girvan, belies a turbulent history. Ayrshire in the late 17th century endured the 'Killing Times' when troops hunted down Covenanters. Straiton was a focus for this unrest and the tomb of one Presbyterian 'martyr' can be found in the village churchyard.

Straiton is believed to derive its name from the Gaelic strath or valley. This walk follows the Water of Girvan south mainly through woods, then returns along the valley floor to the village. A dramatic diversion is via the hill of Craigengower with its summit obelisk that seems to stand sentinel over Straiton. Start from the walkers' car park at

INFORMATION

Distance: 8.5km (5.3 miles) circular.

Start and finish: Walkers' car park, Straiton.

Terrain: Mainly level going on tracks through woodland. Steep climb up grassy slope to Craigengower summit.

Waymarked: Yes.

Refreshments: Inn at Straiton.

Toilets: In Straiton.

Straiton, overlooked by Craigengower

the west end of the village. There is a notice-board and box with leaflets describing the footpath network around the village.

Cross the main road, turn right, then cross a foot-bridge over Lambdoughty Burn. Re-cross the road and join a track that follows the burn south. The track goes through a field, then over a wooden bridge that crosses the Water of Girvan. Continue on to a smaller bridge, then a stile leading to a narrow tarmac road. Turn left and continue to Bennan Farm, then turn right onto a farm track that drops downhill towards a field.

Go through the gate into the field, taking note of the sign that dogs must be on a lead. As you follow the track up through the field, look out for clumps of boulders on the right. These gave a dry base for stacking corn in days before combine harvesters. Turn left at the top of the field and continue to Bennan Wood, entered by a stile over a dyke.

Iron stile by roadside

The wood at this point is a spruce plantation fringed with occasional silver birch. Walk quietly and you may spot a roe deer in the shadows; more noisily and you will flush out a woodpigeon.

About 800m after crossing the stile, leave the track where it swings uphill to the right. Join another track that crosses a boardwalk over a ditch then go through a gate. Here the spruce are replaced by broadleaved trees, mainly oak. Fields grazed by sheep and cattle sweep down to the Water of Girvan, then rise from the opposite bank to the more exposed slopes of Craig Hill and Craigengower.

Continue downhill to Craigfad Farm through occasional muddy stretches. Swing left past the front gate of the whitewashed farmhouse and follow a tarmac road back to the main road. Turn left and walk back towards Straiton—the road is not busy, but watch out for traffic on bends.

On the outskirts of the village, just before the primary school, an iron stile leads over to a field on the right. Follow a track up through the field to the wooded lower slopes of Craigengower. Cross a second stile then follow a track for about 50m to a T-junction beside a waymarker. Turn right and walk about 70m to a second waymarker. Cross a boardwalk and continue uphill for about 200m to a stile over a dyke.

The final climb is steep, so take time to enjoy the view unfolding behind you. At the summit, rest and take in the panorama, stretching from snug little Straiton below to the Christmas pudding form of Ailsa Craig pushing out of the sea off the Ayrshire coast.

Memorial to Lt Col James Hunter Blair on the summit of Craigengower

The granite obelisk on the summit is a memorial to a member of the local gentry, Lt Col James Hunter Blair, who was killed fighting the Russians at the Battle of Inkerman in the Crimean War. The Hunter Blair family remain in the area, at Blairquhan Castle just west of Straiton. This large and grand castle, built in the 1820s, sits in 800 hectares of park and woodland. The castle pays for its keep by being hired out for conferences, weddings and other functions.

Return to the road and head back to Straiton. A wander round the village is well rewarded. Interesting buildings include the Black Bull Inn, with a lintel dated 1766.

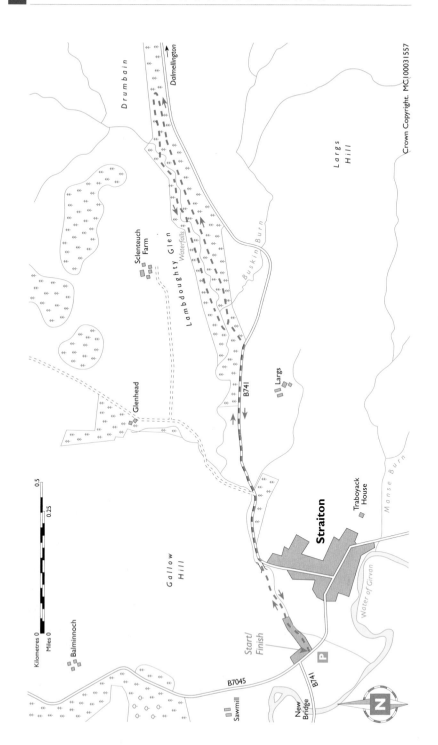

Crown Copyright. MC100031557

LADY HUNTER BLAIR

In Straiton churchyard an old gravestone carries a macabre epitaph: 'Though I was sick and like to die yet Bloody Bruce did murder me because I adhered in my station to our Covenanted Reformation. My blood for vengeance yet doth call upon Zion's haters all.'

The stone is on the grave of Thomas McHaffie, a Covenanter slain in 1686. McHaffie belonged to Largs farm. On the run for two years, he was forced by a bout of influenza to hide closer to home. Eventually his hiding place was discovered by Andrew Bruce, a notorious pursuer of Covenanters. McHaffie, ill and exhausted, sought refuge in a farmhouse outside Straiton, but he was found by Bruce's soldiers and shot. No dragoons ride by Largs farm any more, of course, but many walkers pass the farm entrance on their way to Lady Hunter Blair's walk.

To reach the walk, set off from the walkers' car park at the west end of Straiton. From the car park, cross the road, turn left, then first right into Fowlers Croft. This row of whitewashed cottages and houses with traditional slate roofs looks as though it has been part of Straiton for centuries. It was built in the 1980s, however, and has won a design award for the way it blends in sympathetically with the rest of the village.

Follow a track alongside a low stone wall and small burn that separate Fowlers Croft from fields of grazing sheep. After the last houses, cross the burn by a footbridge and turn left onto the B741 road that leads to Dalmellington, only 8km away.

INFORMATION

Distance: 5km (2.8 miles) circular.

Start and finish: Walkers' car park, Straiton.

Terrain: Pavement and tarmac path past Fowlers Croft to B741 Dalmellington road. This road has relatively little traffic but sensible care must be taken, especially when accompanied by children. Well-surfaced paths through Lambdoughty Glen.

Public transport: Western Buses services to and from Ayr.

Refreshments: Inn at Straiton.

Toilets: In Straiton.

Rossetti's Linn

This quiet road leads gradually uphill, soon passing the entrance to the Straiton–Patna hill track (Walk 9) on the left. Continue uphill, pausing at times to enjoy the unfolding views of Straiton and, further south, Bennan Wood and Craigengower hill with its summit obelisk (Walk 10).

The obelisk is the memorial to James Hunter Blair, who died at the Battle of Inkerman in 1854. His step-mother, Elizabeth, is the Lady Hunter Blair after whom this walk was named. Elizabeth married Sir James Hunter Blair of nearby Blairquhan Castle in the 1840s.

The entrance to Largs Farm is passed on the right and soon after the start to Lady Hunter Blair's walk is reached.

Walking in Lambdoughty Glen

The walk follows well-surfaced paths on either side of wooded Lambdoughty Glen. People wanting a shorter walk may note the car park at the entrance, with a picnic table and a box for walks leaflets. Enter the wood and turn right along the path. Plaques along the way identify different trees such as Sitka spruce, ash and Douglas fir.

The path, well bolstered at vulnerable, steep edges by logs and thick planks, gives a splendid view down through the trees to Lambdoughty Burn. In some places, trees have been blown over the burn. Further up the glen is an attractive 7m waterfall, but further on still is the highlight of this walk—the view down to a 10m high waterfall, the Black Linn or Rossetti's Linn.

The poet Dante Gabriel Rossetti, who helped found the Pre-Raphaelite Brotherhood, visited the glen and is said to have considered suicide at this lovely spot when he felt drawn to the waterfall below. Today, wooden safety barriers have been erected beside steep drops to the burn. A splendidly sited bench overlooks the waterfall. If you sit long enough in the springtime, you might see a duck and her offspring emerge from the undergrowth and venture out onto the rippling water at the base of the fall.

Past Rossetti's Linn, the path runs close to the burn, with water spilling over a series of rock ledges. Cross over the burn by a footbridge. A plaque near the bridge states that this section of path was opened in 1994.

The path rises and falls beside Lambdoughty Burn before eventually crossing a footbridge and climbing up to the entrance to the glen. When you re-enter Straiton, continue down to the main street and turn right to visit the churchyard.

Lambdoughty Burn

Here, another stone, a few feet from Thomas McHaffie's grave, is worthy of study. This is the memorial to James McCosh, a Free Church minister who in the late 1800s became an outstanding president of Princeton University in the United States. McCosh was born at Garsceugh Farm, Patna, close to the Straiton-Patna hill track featured in this guide. The McHaffies are a sept of the Clan McPhee. A John McPhee is an editor of the recent *Princeton Anthology of Writing*. A big world in a small churchyard.

CHANGUE PLANTATION

The conservation village of Barr in South Ayrshire is the centre for more than 30km of walking trails developed by South Ayrshire Council and Scottish Enterprise Ayrshire.

Virtually all of this network of forest paths and roads goes through Changue Plantation, which sprawls across rolling hillside east of the village. The official start for the walks is a car park about 1km east of Barr. At the car park, the trails are described on a notice board and on leaflets in a dispensing box.

Changue Plantation, with mature conifers and broad-leaved trees, provides shelter for a wide variety of birdlife including tits, finches and siskins. This walk, however, may serve as a reminder of how exposed the countryside is beyond the trees.

In January 1913 a young shepherd called Christopher McTaggart set out to tend his flock on the bleak moorland not far from Barr. A snowstorm raged, but Christopher—Kirstie to his family and friends—stuck to his task. Hours later, Kirstie had not returned home. His twin brother and friends searched for Kirstie and eventually found him dying of exposure on the hillside. A few minutes later the 19-year-old passed away, but his body could not be moved until the following day because of the atrocious weather.

A cairn was built to Kirstie's memory on a spot near where he died. This cairn is visited by many walkers who follow Kirstie's Trail, one of the walks in the Barr trails

INFORMATION

Distance: 8.75km (5.4miles) circular.

Start and finish: Walkers' car park, Changue plantation, 1km east of Barr.

Terrain: Forestry roads and tracks. Footwear with good grips on soles recommended for slippy slopes.

Public transport: Western Buses services between Girvan and Barr.

Refreshments: Hotels in Barr.

Toilets: In Barr.

Kirstie's memorial cairn

network. The walk described here is a combination of Kirstie's Trail and the dramatically titled Devil's Trail. The first 500m is shared with Dinmurchie Trail.

From the car park entrance, follow the road away from the village. Just beyond Changue House, Dinmurchie Trail forks up to the right. Take the left fork along the unmetalled road that leads deeper into Changue Plantation. Waymark posts identify Kirstie's Trail in red, the Devil's Trail in purple and Changue Plantation trail in yellow.

Go through a second gate, passing a bench overlooking the Water of Gregg. The road follows the Water of Gregg upriver through a narrow valley. It then crosses the burn and rises through trees, some with bat boxes fixed to their trunks.

Just over 2km from the start, the road passes a purple signpost on the left for the Devil's Trail. Ignore the signpost meantime and continue along the road. About ten minutes later you see the bare hillside beyond the plantation. This is the unsympathetic landscape that the fatally conscientious Kirstie McTaggart found himself in when the blizzard struck.

Walking on the Devil's Trail

The road, which disappears uphill towards the Howe of Laggan, is part of a cycle route that continues east to the Nick of the Balloch hill pass then on to Loch Doon. At the roadside, a red waymarker points right to a path over the burn to the clearing where Kirstie's memorial cairn stands. The clearing is an attractive spot, and walkers can rest and ponder at a picnic table near the cairn.

Walk back down the road to rejoin the Devil's Trail. Follow an attractive grassy track that soon joins a forestry road. Turn left, following a purple arrow, and take the road downhill.

A beautiful view of the Stinchar valley opens up to the north. Then, as the road swings north-east, the whitewashed High Changue farmhouse appears on the opposite hillside.

It was on that hillside, according to legend, that a Laird of Changue agreed to sell his soul to the devil in exchange for great riches. When the devil tried to claim his prize, the Laird reneged. Using his sword to draw a circle around the ground on which they stood, the Laird fought a titanic combat with the devil. Finally, the Laird defeated the devil by throwing him out of the circle.

The mark of the circle and the devil's footprints can still, allegedly, be seen on the hill above High Changue. If you believe such legends, then good luck, because High Changue is the next landmark on the walk. The road climbs uphill then reaches another purple sign that points left towards a grassy slope that leads down to the Changue Burn. Take care on the downhill track because it can be slippy when wet.

Walking to Kirstie's cairn

At the foot of the slope, a footbridge crosses the burn. The track leads uphill, passes through a wood then joins a forestry road that runs east to join the road past Kirstie's cairn. Turn left down the road, passing High Changue farm and an attractive avenue of beech trees, and arrive back at the car park.

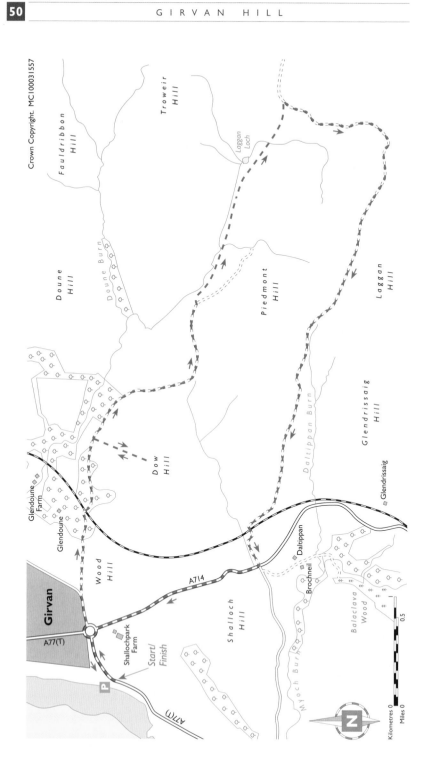

Crown Copyright. MCI0003I557

GIRVAN HILL

If you ever go across the sea to Ireland, one of the routes to follow is the A77 trunk road from Glasgow to the ferry port of Stranraer.

Some 56 miles (90km) south of Glasgow, motorists come to the town of Girvan that sits on the Carrick coast in the southwest corner of Ayrshire. One very attractive feature of Girvan—the harbour—is missed by through traffic. But motorists cannot fail to notice another: the line of green, craggy hills that form an impressive backdrop to the town.

This walk heads up into those hills along easy but often boggy tracks. These tracks provide outstanding views down to Girvan and out across the sea to the granite dome of Ailsa Craig.

From the centre of Girvan, go south along the main street to Shalloch Park roundabout. Motorists should take the third exit, signposted A77 Stranraer. After about 200 metres, turn right into the large car park beside a sandy beach. Here are public toilets, a walks display board and (in summer) an ice cream stand. The route you follow is the blue one called Laggan Walk.

Walk back to the roundabout and take the second exit (the first exit if you are walking from town), signposted 'Ayr Avoiding Low Bridge'. Alternatively, you can take the train from Glasgow, an enjoyable ride, and walk from the station to the roundabout to join the walk.

INFORMATION

Distance: 9km (5.625 miles) circular.

Start and finish: Seashore car park near Shalloch Park roundabout, Girvan.

Terrain: Short distance on pavements. Most of walk on good tracks that, however, may be boggy after heavy rain or in areas churned up by sheep and walkers. Stout footwear, including wellingtons, recommended—especially after heavy rain.

Public transport: Regular direct rail services between Glasgow Central and Girvan via Kilmarnock and Ayr (very limited on Sundays). Western Bus services between Ayr and Stranraer.

Refreshments: Wide selection of cafes and bars in Girvan.

Toilets: At seashore car park.

View to Girvan

Continue for about 100 metres and cross to the right-hand side of the road where there is a gate beside a sign for the Girvan to Barr Hill Path. This path is a right of way that crosses 11 km of grassy moorland before arriving (naturally) at the village of Barr, also featured in this book. Go through the gate and follow a farm track uphill towards a deciduous wood. The track goes through the wood, often loud with birdsong, passes a gate displaying a faded marker arrow to Glen Doune, then swings right to cross an old stone railway bridge. A short distance ahead, cross a stile then exit the wood by a gate and cattle grid.

The track steepens, passing the open slopes of Dow Hill on the right. The summit, soon reached from the track, is the site of an ancient fort. It is also an excellent vantage point with views north to the Firth of Clyde and south to neighbouring Byne Hill.

View to Byne Hill

To the north of Girvan you can now see the ISP Alginates plant where food ingredients are produced from brown seaweed. Ayrshire is so famous for its food products, particularly dairy produce, that Nestlé set up a plant at Girvan to turn out milk-based products for its confectionery.

The track continues climbing for about 500 metres, passes through a gate then gradually narrows and heads south-eastwards. Waymarkers bearing red and blue arrows provide reassurance on faint stretches through long grass.

The route eventually passes through a drystone dyke and fords a stream. Cut straight across boggy, reedy ground. Do not be misled by a solitary post standing over to the left among the reeds; this is not a waymarker, just an old fence remnant. Also to the left, a clump of trees conceals tiny, circular Loch Laggan.

Beyond the reedy ground, the track eventually joins a broader farm track. Here, turn left and walk up the facing hillside to catch sight of the loch. Now look to the south-east to see where the farm track follows the side of a valley along a further stretch of the Girvan–Barr Hill Path. Both communities are typical of towns and villages around Ayrshire where local councils, Scottish Enterprise Ayrshire, landowners and ALERT (Ayrshire Local Enterprise Resources Trust, headed by the ever-enthusiastic David Gray) are working together to create networks of walking paths backed up by excellent leaflets.

It is now time to head back to the coast. Follow the farm track south towards Laggan Hill. Before it reaches that hill, the track turns north-west and passes through a gate and sheep folds before dropping steeply to the railway line beside the A714 Girvan-Barrhill road.

Ailsa Craig from hill track

On the descent, you can enjoy the view south to Byne Hill and, once again, Ailsa Craig. In the evening haze, the rock seems to hover above the water like a bowler hat in a Magritte painting. From Girvan, a fishing port and popular holiday resort, there are organised boat trips to the island, which has a large gannet colony.

The track passes through an arch below the railway line and joins the A714. At the road, turn right and walk back to the Shalloch Park roundabout.

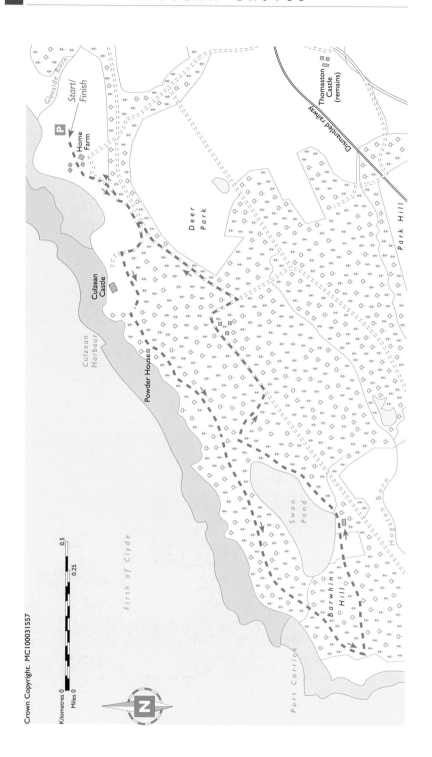

Crown Copyright. MCI00031557

Kilometres 0
Miles 0
0.25
0.5

N

Glenside Burn

Start/
Finish

P

Home
Farm

Deer
Park

Culzean
Harbour

Culzean
Castle

Powder House

Firth of Clyde

Port Carrick

Swan
Pond

Barwhin Hill

Hogston Burn

Park Hill

Dismantled railway

Thomaston
Castle
(remains)

CULZEAN CASTLE

Some places are too famous for their own good. They receive so much praise that when you get there, they fail to come up to expectations. Culzean Castle is not one of those places. Ayrshire's most celebrated building makes a stunning impression in a spectacular setting.

In the late 1770s, the 10th Earl of Cassillis asked the renowned Scottish architect Robert Adam to enlarge the existing castle that stood on a cliff jutting into the Firth of Clyde. Adam created a romantic masterpiece. The castle, now owned by the National Trust for Scotland, attracts thousands of visitors each year. Visitors can pay to view the castle, the 531-acre country park, or both. In 2003, admission to the park was £13.50 per family (NTS members free).

Culzean (pronounced Cullayne) Castle can be reached by the A719 coast road south from Ayr. The country park is well signposted, and guides issued at the main entrance show clearly the wide choice of paths to follow.

This walk begins at the visitor centre, in the Adam-designed Home Farm. This group of buildings, including a restaurant and shop, forms a square enclosing a courtyard. An archway stands at each corner.

Leave the courtyard through the archway nearest the clifftop; a sign points to the castle.

Pause beyond the archway to enjoy a view of the castle perched on its rock. Out to sea sits the island of Arran, with Goatfell and neighbouring mountains displaying their famous 'sleeping warrior' profile. Further south, the pudding-bowl shape of Ailsa Craig rises from the water.

INFORMATION

Distance: 4.75km (2.8 miles) circular.

Start and finish: Visitor centre at Home Farm.

Terrain: Well-surfaced paths and tracks. Steep tracks to shore.

Public Transport: Western Buses services between Ayr-Maidens go past castle entrance.

Refreshments: Self-service restaurant at visitor centre.

Toilets: At the visitor centre.

Opening hours: Country park open every day. Castle open daily Easter to late October, 1000-1700, plus weekends in November and December. Restaurant open as Castle, plus weekends from January to March.

Visitors passing under Adam's archway

Follow signs to the castle. The main approach, a stone viaduct over a ravine, is guarded by a mock-ruined arch. This piece of romanticism was possibly inspired by ancient buildings that Adam saw on his Grand Tour in Italy.

Culzean Castle from the Fountain Court

Stone steps lead down to the beautiful Fountain Court. This formal garden gives a view of the front of the castle. The fountain was restored in the late 1990s. The NTS has raised millions of pounds over the years to restore the castle and other buildings on the estate. The fine condition of the estate is testament to this fundraising work and the careful way in which restoration has been carried out.

Walk through the Fountain Court, then climb a stone staircase and exit through an archway to join the west green battery. Here, a row of cannon remains dug in, still awaiting an attack by Napoleon's fleet.

From the battery, follow signs for the Cliff Walk. This trail follows woodland paths high above the shoreline. Care must be taken with youngsters because there are steep drops close to the path. There are obvious routes down to the shore, particularly one, before the Powder House, that gives firm footing on a boardwalk.

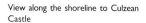

View along the shoreline to Culzean Castle

By the gravelly beach near the boardwalk are the old laundry, now an outdoor education centre, and a pepper-pot shaped building once used as a bathers' changing room. Back on the clifftop, you soon reach the Powder House, used to store gunpowder for a gun that gave a morning wake-up call.

The Cliff Walk gives splendid views north to the castle and south to Ailsa Craig and the lighthouse at Turnberry Point. The path eventually swings inland towards the Swan Pond. Just before the pond, fork right towards the small cove of Port Carrick. A short distance on, a path leads easily down to the sandy beach, a paradise for youngsters.

A short distance further on lies heather-clad Barwhin Hill. From here you can see the large sandy beach at Maidens. The path swings downhill to a fork where you can turn right to the beach. Turn left and enter the woodland to return to the Swan Pond.

Pagoda in the woods

Soon, a pagoda appears through the trees. This was built in 1814 by the castle's owners, the Kennedys, to house exotic birds and animals. Further on the Swan Pond shimmers in the sunlight. Ducks paddle busily and mute swans glide serenely over the water.

Walk past the Swan Pond Centre. Follow the path at the pond's edge to a wooden bird-watching hide on stilts. Here swans can be viewed on an island nesting site.

Just beyond the pond, the castle's ice house lies hidden in the trees. Follow a right fork in the path uphill to a tarmac road. Turn left and walk past the walled garden. Follow this road round some bends and past the ornate Camelia House on the left.

Just after the Camelia House, fork left towards Culzean Castle. This path ends at steps that lead up to the viaduct and the Ruined Arch. Return to the visitor centre, where the café may well be a welcome sight.

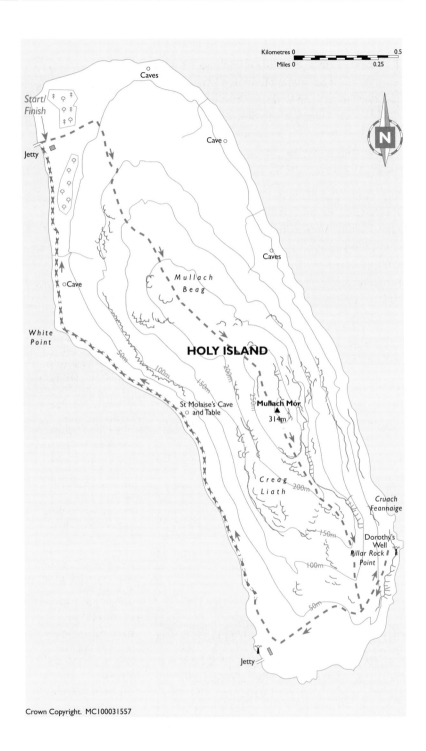

Kilometres 0   0.5
Miles 0   0.25

Caves

*Start/
Finish*

Jetty

Cave

Cave

Caves

*Mullach
Beag*

*White
Point*

HOLY ISLAND

▲ **Mullach Mór**
314m

St Molaise's Cave
and Table

*Creag
Liath*

200m

*Cruach
Feannaige*

Dorothy's
Well

*Pillar Rock
Point*

150m

100m

50m

50m

100m

150m

200m

Jetty

HOLY ISLE

Like a Buddhist prayer wheel, Holy Isle's history has come full circle. Holy Isle ('Island' seems mainly used on Ordnance Survey maps) first achieved prominence in the 6th century when it was believed to have been the place of retreat for a Celtic monk, St Molaise. Today, it is once more a centre for religious worship, in this case Buddhism.

Holy Isle was purchased in 1992 by the Samye Ling Tibetan Centre, which is based at Eskdalemuir in Dumfriesshire. Visitors are welcome, but they must conform to five 'golden rules', which include protecting life, speaking the truth, respecting other people and their property, and refraining from tobacco, drink and drugs.

The Holy Isle community has planted thousands of native trees and nurtures rare livestock breeds including Soay sheep and Eriskay ponies.

Visitors can walk on the island so long as they follow designated paths and do not enter areas where religious meditation may be taking place. During the 2001 foot and mouth crisis, the island was re-opened to visitors before many other restricted areas in Scotland.

Holy Isle rises like a whale's back from the sea, almost sealing off Lamlash Bay from the Firth of Clyde. King Haakon of Norway sheltered his galley fleet in the bay before his defeat at the Battle of

INFORMATION

Distance: 7.5km (4.8 miles) circular.

Start and finish: Jetty at north end of Holy Isle.

Terrain: Walking boots recommended. Rough and sometimes boggy ground over summit ridge. Mild scrambling at saddle and on descent from Mullach Beag. Excellent shore paths and tracks.

Public Transport: Good links make a day visit to Holy Isle possible from the mainland, especially in summer. Regular train service between Glasgow Central Station and Ardrossan Harbour. Regular 55-minute CalMac ferry service between Ardrossan Harbour and Brodick. On Arran, Western Buses and Royal Mail post buses provide scheduled services between Brodick and Lamlash. Regular ferry service from old pier at Lamlash (hourly from Easter to end August, less frequent in other months.) For information phone 01770 600998.

Refreshments: Wide choice of pubs and cafes in Lamlash and Brodick.

Toilets: In Lamlash.

Holy Isle from Clauchland Hills

Largs in 1263. Last century, the Royal Navy's Home Fleet paid visits. And, sadly, Lamlash Bay was the embarcation point for Arran families cleared off the land in 1829 to make way for agricultural improvements.

Today Lamlash Bay is filled with yachts. A small launch ferries visitors between Lamlash and Holy Isle. When the launch ties up at the jetty at the island's north end, a community member greets visitors and explains the attractions and rules of Holy Isle.

This walk starts from the jetty. Follow the drystone wall towards the old farmhouse, home to volunteers. At the end of the wall, turn left and follow a track across the neighbouring field to a wooden gate. Climb the gate and follow the track uphill through bracken to a barbed-wire fence. Climb a stile and continue uphill, observing the 'Please Keep to Path' sign.

The climb is rewarded with a view over Lamlash Bay. Keep going uphill, ignoring a track that contours right, below a small outcrop. The uphill track reaches Mullach Beag, the first top on the summit

Looking north from the summit of Mullach Mor

Pillar Rock lighthouse

ridge of Holy Isle. The view is truly remarkable. On a sunny day, the Christmas pudding shape of Ailsa Craig is seen to the south, sitting stolidly in the shimmering water.

From Mullach Beag the track descends to a saddle, then rises steeply towards the island's summit, the 314-metre Mullach Mor. The start of the climb from the saddle involves scrambling over a couple of awkward steps, but hand and footholds are plentiful.

Mullach Mor, with its triangulation pillar, is another wonderful viewpoint. Look out for goats grazing on the slopes below. The island is also rich in birdlife that includes curlew, gulls, cormorants and guillemots.

The path downhill to the south end of the island is awkward in places, passing over several rocky steps and smooth slabs. Again, holds are plentiful. Signs warning 'Danger Crevasses Ahead' should be heeded; these refer to several deep rock clefts half-hidden in the heather beside the path.

At the shore path, turn left to walk to the square-shaped Pillar Rock lighthouse at the south-east corner of the island. The rugged east shore of the island can be viewed by passing through a gate beside the lighthouse and walking down a grassy track.

Walk back along the shore path, passing the junction with the summit track, and head down towards the island's other lighthouse. On the hillside above stands the retreat master's cabin.

Buddhist painting

At the end of a field, beside cottages and a walled garden, a row of small standing stones displays Buddhist inscriptions. This is a foretaste of the rather exotic final leg to the jetty. The grassy path up the western shoreline passes several rock faces decorated with bright, pastel-coloured paintings of Buddhist saints. Prayer flags attached to branches washed up on the rocks flap lazily in the wind.

About halfway along this stretch, a branch path leads to a small cave believed to have been where St Molaise lived as a hermit. Molaise is thought to have been born in Argyll but trained in Ireland.

St Molaise's Cave

Holy Isle was originally known as Eilean Molaise, Gaelic for Molaise's Island. This became Elmolaise, Limolas, and finally Lamlash, the name of course given to the village across the bay.

When the Tibetan Centre bought Holy Isle, an ecumenical service was held at the cave to mark the community's commitment to the island's spiritual heritage.

The excellent path continues north, overshadowed by crags, before arriving back at the jetty.

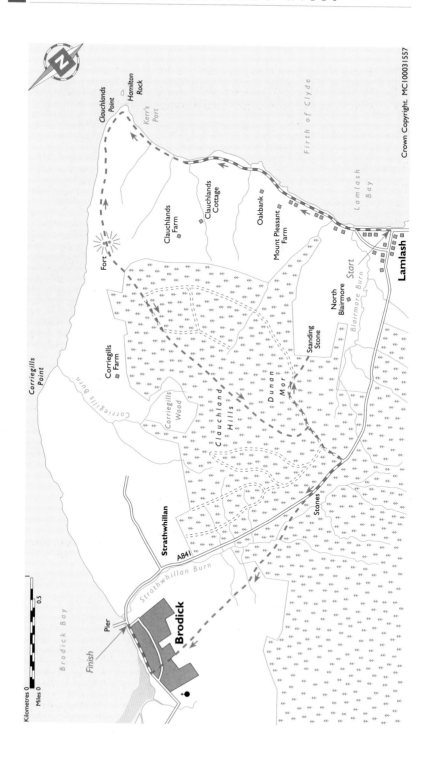

Crown Copyright. MC100031557

THE CLAUCHLAND HILLS

The Clauchland Hills throw a protective arm around two of Arran's most important anchorages, the bays at Lamlash and Brodick. Rising to only 260 metres, the hills offer genuinely wonderful views in exchange for moderate effort. This walk starts at Lamlash, goes to Clauchlands Point, follows the crest of the ridge formed by the Clauchland Hills, and then descends by the coast road and a woodland track to Brodick.

From the centre of Lamlash, join the road that runs northeast by the shoreline to Clauchlands Point. The road passes houses that command fine views across Lamlash Bay to Holy Isle, and a derelict church where only pigeons congregate.

When the road swings left to Clauchlands Farm, cross a stile beside a gate and follow a track that continues the way by the shore.

The often-boggy track passes a wartime pillbox with a commanding view of Lamlash Bay, then continues a short distance towards the point. Just off the shore is Hamilton Rock, a low, rocky perch for seabirds such as shags and gulls.

Follow a track that runs north into the mouth of a small quarry, then rises right to pass a second pillbox. Continue uphill for about 200 metres and climb over an old iron gate.

Follow a track uphill through bracken. A fence on the left separates the track from fields that rise up the slope to meet the plantation that caps the Clauchland Hills. To the right of the track, cliffs drop down to the shore.

INFORMATION

Distance: 13km (8miles) linear.

Start: Lamlash.

Finish: Brodick.

Terrain: Stout footwear with good treads recommended. Muddy stretches on track to Clauchlands Point and across Clauchland Hills. Steep climb to Iron Age fort, and rough descent to standing stone.

Public Transport: Western Buses and Royal Mail post buses provide regular scheduled services between Brodick and Lamlash.

Refreshments: Wide variety of pubs and cafes in Brodick and Lamlash.

Toilets: In Lamlash and Brodick.

View north to Goatfell from Dun Fionn

The track continues uphill to a knoll with a triangulation pillar on its summit. This knoll is Dun Fionn, site of a fort built during the Iron Age which began about 2,500 years ago. It is easy to see why anyone should have sought refuge here. Dun Fionn is well protected by steep slopes on its landward sides and cliffs on the seaward side. There are outstanding views both inland and along the coastline, making this a splendid site for a picnic.

The view south is dominated by Holy Isle. The view north draws the eye across attractive farmland to the entrance to Brodick Bay. On the northern skyline sits Arran's tallest mountain, Goatfell, and its neighbouring peaks.

From Dun Fionn, walk down the steep slope and follow the track that heads west to the plantation. At the edge of the trees, ignore a track that branches right towards Brodick. Instead, climb a stile into the plantation and follow the track uphill.

Forestry plantations can often be uninspiring places to walk through. This is not the case with Clauchland Hills. The heather-clad crest of the ridge is bare of trees, so ever-changing panoramas can be enjoyed along the way.

Goatfell and CalMac ferry *Caledonian Isles* from Clauchland Hills

The track initially twists and turns through the trees until it reaches the crest where the gradient eases off. At one point, two Norway spruce stand

on either side of the track, forming a welcoming gateway. The friendly atmosphere of the place is not dispelled even when you reach the top of the final slope and find a raven perched on the summit cairn.

The walk along the ridge gives an expanding view of Brodick, its bay, its castle and the hills beyond. If your timing is right you might see the CalMac ferry *Caledonian Isles* carving a wake through the water.

Follow the track downhill until you eventually come to a large, bracken-filled clearing. At the bottom of the clearing, join a track forking to the left, marked with a sign for 'Cairn and Standing Stone'. The track crosses a small burn and continues for about 400 metres to Dunan Mor cairn, the remains of a chambered tomb.

Standing stone in the woods

Beyond the cairn, the track runs steeply downhill over rough ground, passes through a tunnel of trees and finally emerges in a clearing occupied by a standing stone. This 2m tall stone appears to have some carvings on its downhill face. Return to the junction of the paths and turn left to follow a forestry road towards the main coast road between Lamlash and Brodick. Trees have been harvested in this area, and the smell of pine resin on a warm day is a tonic.

Near the junction with the main road, a stone circle can be seen to the right, through a gap in the trees. At the main road, turn right and walk towards Brodick. After about 500m, on a long downhill stretch, a sign marks the start of a footpath to Brodick. Cross the road and follow the path as it wends downhill towards the town. The final stretch is along a charming lane, or cart track as they are known on Arran.

The lane emerges on the main road through Brodick, with the pier to your right.

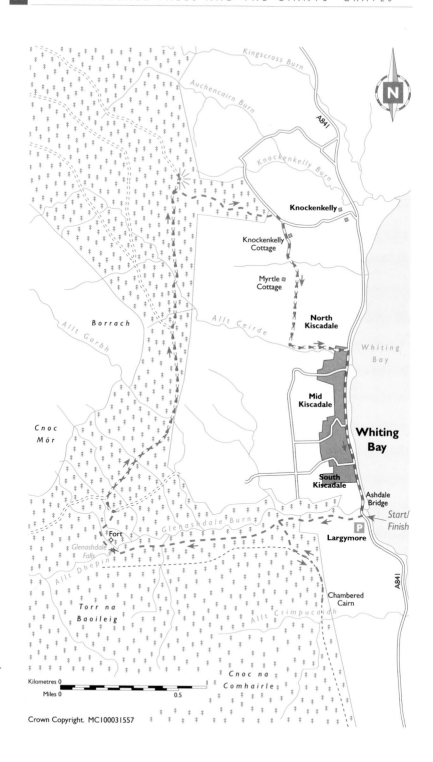

Crown Copyright. MC100031557

GLENASHDALE FALLS AND THE GIANTS' GRAVES

Prehistoric burial chambers in a secluded woodland clearing. A dramatic waterfall that tumbles down a lovely glen. A 'homeward' stroll along a pretty country lane.

What more could a body ask for on a walk? There is a price to pay, however, for enjoying Glenashdale. The walk from the shoreline at Whiting Bay involves some steep climbing, particularly up one woodland stairway with more than 300 steps. But then that's all the more reason to take your time and enjoy delightful surroundings.

Whiting Bay is a popular tourist village that is strung out along more than 2km of Arran's eastern shore. This walk starts at Ashdale Bridge, which is at the south end of the village, beside the Youth Hostel, where Glenashdale Burn flows into Whiting Bay.

Follow a narrow lane that runs between the hostel and the burn. This lane, bordered by wild flowers, is signposted to the Giants' Graves. You soon enter a broadleaved woodland where, in summer, a pungent smell of wild garlic hangs in the air. The walk is now along a path that shortly divides, with signposts indicating right to Glenashdale Falls and left to the Giants' Caves.

Take the left fork and head uphill into a mature conifer plantation. The climb steepens at the staircase; pause to look up and see how the sun filters through the trees. Take your time up the long flight of steps.

INFORMATION

Distance: 9.25km (5.75 miles) circular.

Start and finish: Ashdale Bridge, beside Whiting Bay Youth Hostel.

Terrain: Forest paths, very steep or muddy in places, forestry roads and country lanes.

Public Transport: Western Buses and Royal Mail post buses provide scheduled services to and from Brodick and other coastal communities.

Refreshments: Wide range in Whiting Bay.

Toilets: In Whiting Bay.

The Giants' Graves

The steps end near a picnic table. Turn left and follow a broad path uphill, pausing along the way to read plaques on the tree trunks. The plaques identify non-native species such as sycamore and lodgepole pine. Stop also where trees have been cleared to show Whiting Bay and Holy Isle.

The path follows a dark tunnel through the trees, then emerges into a grassy clearing flooded in light. This is the site of the Giants' Graves. Far from being the last resting place of mythical heroes, these large stone slabs formed burial cairns that contained the bodies of people living in the Neolithic or New Stone Age period, at least 4,000 years ago.

Neolithic people had learned to fashion stone axe-heads by grinding or polishing rather than by chipping. As a result they were better equipped to clear land for cultivation. As there was only a limited number of places that produced good-quality stone for axe-heads, trading was extensive. Axe-heads from Antrim and Great Langdale in the Lake District were especially prized on Arran and elsewhere in Scotland.

Return to the main path and take the fork signposted to Glenashdale Falls. The path to the falls is less steep than the one to the Giants' Graves, but it is muddy in several places. As the path rises above Glenashdale Burn, conifers give way to broadleaved trees including birch, ash and alder.

Glenashdale Falls

Higher up, the sound of rushing water tells you that the falls are nearby. Just before the falls, a path branches down to a viewing platform where the falls can be seen plunging more than 30 metres down a narrow gorge. At the time of writing, access to the viewing platform was barred for safety reasons, because of damage caused by trees blown down in the 1998 Boxing Day storm.

As you continue the climb you can see where Forest Enterprise has cleared a lot of trees that blocked the main path. Soon you cross the burn by a wooden bridge. Here, the contrast with the falls could hardly be greater. Glenashdale Burn flows gently through shallow rock pools. A picnic bench and a view of Whiting Bay guarantees a delightful rest after the climb.

Continue along the path, go through a gap in a stone dyke then take the right fork, signposted Whiting Bay via Iron Age Fort. The scattered rock remains of this fort are soon reached, on a site commanding a broad view southwards.

Cart track to Whiting Bay

The path soon passes a bench at another falls viewpoint, then joins a forestry road. This road can take you directly down to Whiting Bay. Turn left, however, and walk up to a junction with another forestry road. Turn right, following a sign for Lamlash, and walk along the forestry road for just over 1 km to a picnic table opposite an area of bulldozed ground. The table gives an outstanding view of Lamlash Bay and Holy Isle.

Retrace your steps for about 100 metres, then follow a path downhill, marked Whiting Bay via Hawthorne. This path runs under a canopy of trees to a tarmac road that serves cottages. Turn right and follow this road, which becomes an unmetalled lane flanked by grassy banks and hedges. The lane soon joins the shore road north of the main village car park for the return to Ashdale Bridge.

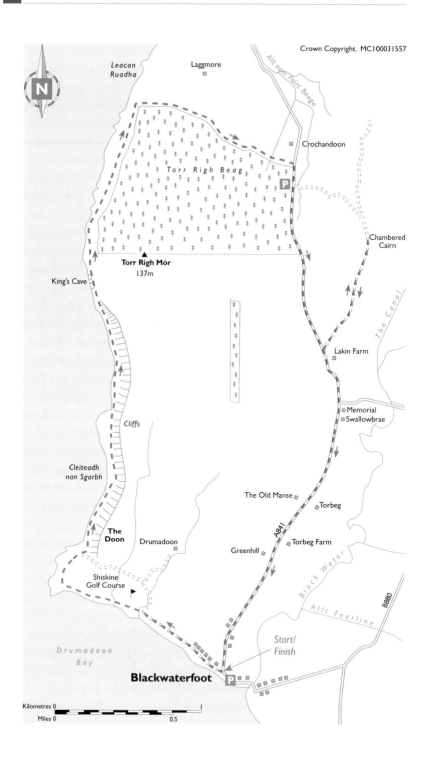

Crown Copyright. MC100031557

THE KING'S CAVE

The popular seaside village of Blackwaterfoot sits on the south-west corner of Arran. The village with its tiny, picturesque harbour looks across Kilbrannan Sound to the Kintyre peninsula, only 10km away. This fascinating walk from Blackwaterfoot takes in geology, prehistory and one of Scotland's most famous legends along the way. The first section of the walk runs north for just over 1km along a lovely beach.

Go on to the beach near the golf course, and walk along the sands towards Drumadoon Point. On the right, dunes conceal the golf course, and on the beach, dykes of igneous rock (molten rock which has solidified) run across the sand and into the sea. Oystercatchers strut along the shore and cormorants gather on the low, rocky Drumadoon Point to air their wings before setting off for another plunge into the sea for fish.

The beach ends at the point. The route then follows a grassy path between the shoreline and the edge of the golf course. Looming ahead is the impressive Doon cliff, made up of hexagonal columns

INFORMATION

Distance: 10.75km (6.7 miles) circular.

Start and Finish: The beach at Blackwaterfoot.

Terrain: Beach walk, narrow tracks below cliffs and along foreshore, well surfaced path skirting plantation, and boggy track to burial cairn.

Public Transport: Western Buses and Royal Mail post buses provide scheduled services to and from Brodick and other coastal communities.

Refreshments: Hotels at Blackwaterfoot.

Toilets: In Blackwaterfoot.

Igneous dyke crossing the beach near Blackwaterfoot

of igneous rock. The view north reveals King's Cave and its neighbouring caves.

Arran has an important place in the history of geology. In the late 18th century an Edinburgh scientist, Dr James Hutton, discovered a place on the island where successive rock layers had been laid down. This confounded the Creation Theory that the earth was formed in a short time. His book *A Theory of the Earth*, first published in 1785, formed the basis of modern geology. Arran's wide variety of rocks and rock formations means that the island is still an important destination for geology students.

To reach the Doon, follow the path between boulders then through a cleft in a rock outcrop. Skirt round the golf course to reach a fence. Cross a stile then follow a path up to the cliff.

On the path beneath the Doon's hexagonal basalt columns

At this point a rock stack or tower leans out from the cliff. On top of the Doon, sheep graze on the site of a large iron age fort.

The path hugs the base of the cliff as it crosses above steep grassy slopes that roll down to the rocky shore. At the end of the cliff, the path divides. The right branch climbs to the top of the Doon, with a good view of Drumadoon Point. The left branch leads across flat grassy ground to the striking row of white sandstone pillars at the entrance to King's Cave and its neighbours.

Dramatic sandstone caves

The long row of caves looks like bleached skulls in an elephants' graveyard. The caves were formed about 6,000 years ago when the sea was higher. King's Cave is the cavern with the deepest recess, guarded by an iron gate. This cave is thought to have been one of the places where Robert the Bruce hid before he returned to the mainland and defeated the English army at Bannockburn in 1314. According to legend, it was here that the Bruce was inspired to fight on when he saw the spider 'try, try and try again' to build its web. Another legend says that the Irish giant Fingal stayed in the cave during hunting trips to Arran. A key to the gate is available from Brodick tourist information centre.

Continue north along a shingle bank for about 100 metres, then join a track that crosses a stile and goes through a rocky cleft. This track joins a well-surfaced path that rises above the shore, skirting a plantation on the right. Ahead lies Machrie Bay, its waters shimmering blue on a

Chambered cairn near Torbeg

sunny day, and the 721m peak of Beinn Bharrain further north.

The path curves round the edge of the plantation and arrives at a Forest Enterprise car park beside the A841 coast road. At the road, turn right and walk south for about 1.5km. Just before the Torbeg boundary sign, turn left down a track. Follow this track for about 600 metres through two gates and across some boggy ground until you reach moorland. Ahead stands a group of boulders, the remains of a chambered burial cairn more than 4,000 years old. To the north is the desolate expanse of Machrie Moor with its famous groups of standing stones (Walk 19).

Return to the road and continue the walk back to Blackwaterfoot. At the tur-off to Shiskine stands an interesting roadside monument to a local 19th century Free Church minister, the Rev. Archibald Nicol, 'a man of sterling worth'.

The rest of the walk gives pleasant views to Shiskine, and finally, down to the buildings and harbour huddled round the Black Water that gives this pretty village its name.

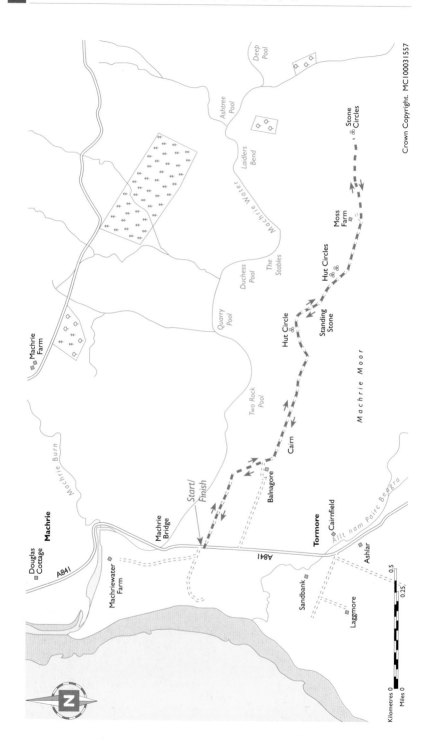

Crown Copyright. MC100031557

MACHRIE MOOR

What is a short stroll doing in a book like this? A four-kilometre there-and-back amble along a farm track and over boggy ground can hardly be described as exercise. But that is not the point of Machrie Moor. If you were to equate this to today's corporate world of leisure and recreation, the walk would be more a thoughtful wander round an art gallery than a strenuous bout of circuit training.

It is in that vein that people from all over the world visit Machrie Moor to see its stone circles. Why else should strangers squeeze their cars onto a grass verge then set off across a field in the drizzle? Not that it drizzles all the time on Arran. Not at all, but rain and mist seem to add to the atmosphere of such prehistoric sites.

The stone monuments of Machrie Moor are not as well known as, for instance, those at Callanish on the island of Lewis. Nevertheless Aubrey Burl, the distinguished writer on archaeology, describes the monuments on Machrie Moor as possibly the best group of architecturally varied stone circles in Western Europe.

INFORMATION

Distance: 4km (2.5 miles) circular.
Start and finish: Lay-by and field entrance on A841 coast road about 5km north of Blackwaterfoot (GR895330).
Terrain: Field and moorland tracks, boggy in places.
Public Transport: Western Buses and Royal Mail post buses provide scheduled services to and from Brodick and other coastal communities.
Refreshments: Hotel at Blackwaterfoot.

Standing stone with remnant believed to have been damaged in an attempt to turn it into a millstone

The district of Machrie lies on the west coast of Arran, a short distance north of the attractive seaside village of Blackwaterfoot. Machrie itself has a small settlement strung along the shore. One attraction in the area is the 9-hole golf course with views across Kilbrannan Sound to the Mull of Kintyre.

From Blackwaterfoot, travel north along the A841 coast road. Go past the right turn for Shiskine and continue for about 2.5km to Machrie Moor. Signs give motorists adequate warning that they are approaching the stones. Nevertheless great care must be taken by drivers because this stretch of the coast road runs between high verges, and parking is restricted. There is an area for cars on the left side of the road beside a field entrance, but please park well clear of the gate.

Wooden walkway leading to a stone circle

Cross the road and enter the field opposite, waymarked to the standing stones, by a stile. Follow a track across the field. Beyond a second stile lies the Moss Farm Road Stone Circle. A single line of granite boulders forms the circle inside which was found the remains of a burial cairn. This circle dates from the Bronze Age, about 2,000-1,500BC.

After the circle, the ground becomes more boggy and moorlike. Continue on, crossing a third stile beside a derelict farm. The ground now falls away to the moor. Walkers will have already seen several ancient monuments on both sides of the track. But now, just after the farm, the sight they will see is extraordinary.

Stone circle on Machrie Moor

Groups of stones stand like sentinels in the bleak moorland. Particularly striking are several tall red sandstone pillars. Also in this area are lower rings created with boulders. The approach to the standing stones is very boggy, so sleepers have been laid on the track to make the walking a little easier.

Excavations on Machrie Moor have found traces of hut circles. Remains date back to the Neolithic and Bronze ages, between 5,500 and 3,000 years ago. Excellent information boards, placed by Historic Scotland which cares for the monuments, describe the scene in great detail. But what the boards cannot do is unravel the mystery of what purpose the stones and rings served for their builders. Another mystery is how people with simple tools managed to move such huge objects. Presumably they had learnt the technique of using rope, rollers and levers, but that does not detract from the scale of their achievements.

It is fascinating to wander round the stones and circles and approach them from different angles, to see them in relation to the landscape. Machrie Moor, at the time that these stones were erected, would have been a more hospitable place, with cultivation going on.

By the time the visit ends, a lot more time might have passed than you might expect from a walk of little over a mile. The return over the same track gives an opportunity to look at stone circles that you might have missed on the outward leg.

Standing stones on Machrie Moor

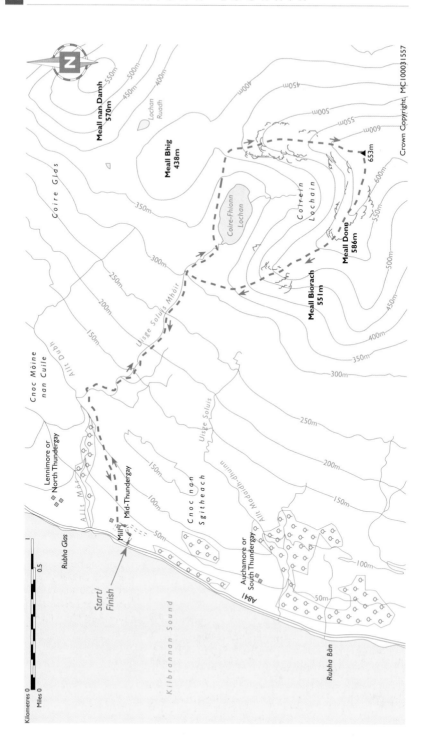

FHIONN LOCHAIN

This walk is one of the shorter outings in the book, yet it possibly gives the greatest sense of solitude.

Fhionn Lochain—or Fhion Lochain depending on whose map you read—hides in the hills at the north-west corner of Arran. Reasonably fit people will find the lochan is very accessible, however, because it is less than 3km from the tiny settlement of Mid Thundergay. Young children might also be able to make the walk to the lochan if they are tempted with a picnic on a sunny day on its attractive, granite sand beaches.

Visitors will reach Mid Thundergay by the A841 coast road. Cars can be parked beside the turnoff for Mid Thundergay, announced by signs for Coirein Lochain.

A short walk takes you to the picturesque cottages that make up Mid Thundergay. An unmetalled road then wends its way up between the houses until you are confronted by two gates. Go through the right-hand gate, which may have an old wooden sign for the lochan.

Follow a faint track up through a field, keeping close to the fence on the left. A short distance on, the track becomes more bouldery and obvious when it passes through an area of bracken. Beyond the bracken, go over a deer fence by a stile.

INFORMATION

Distance: 8 km (5.2 miles) circular.

Start and finish: Mid Thundergay on A841 coast road, north-west Arran.

Terrain: Short but challenging hill walk. Track to Fhionn Lochain muddy, steep and rocky in places. Beyond the lochan, ridge walk with steep descent back to track. Hill walking boots recommended.

Public transport: Western Buses and Royal Mail post buses provide scheduled services to and from Brodick and other coastal communities. There is also a car ferry service to Lochranza from Claonaig in Kintyre.

Refreshments: Hotels at Catacol and Lochranza. The Isle of Arran Distillery, Lochranza, has a visitor centre with restaurant.

Opening hours: Isle of Arran Distillery, daily 1000-1600 Apr-Oct; for winter hours phone 01770 830264

View from the ridge down to Fhionn Lochain

The track heads uphill through heather roughly in the direction of Meall nan Damh, the prominent rounded summit to the north-east. Cross over a small burn by stepping stones, beside birch trees, then turn right to join a second burn.

Follow the second burn, Uisge Soluis Mhoir, up-hill in the direction of Meall Biorach. This steep-sided hill is part of the ridge that forms a climax to this walk because it overlooks Fhionn Lochain. Uisge Soluis Mhoir flows out of Fhionn Lochain. The track follows the course of the burn uphill, sometimes crossing the burn at shallow points, but staying clear of several small waterfalls along the way. It becomes more rutted and bouldery as it gains height. There is a big compensation, though, in the expanding view across Kilbrannan Sound to Kintyre.

The track to Fhionn Lochain, with cone-shaped Meall Biorach in background

Eventually, the track crests the rise and Fhionn Lochain appears before you. On a sunny day, this is an idyllic spot. The lochan sits cradled in the corrie or coire named after it. Coire is Gaelic for cauldron, the description given to a mountain cirque, or hollow, carved out by ice. When clouds roll in, the corrie can indeed look like a sinister, steaming cauldron. The possible threat of poor visibility and bad weather can quickly chase away idyllic impressions of Coire Fhionn Lochain.

Anyone visiting Fhionn Lochain should carry a map and compass and know how to use them, if only to identify landmarks on a clear day. Although the track is easy to follow in bad weather, it should be remembered that it does go through mountain terrain.

This walk becomes more serious if you decide to walk round the top of the corrie. Although the height gained and distance walked is moderate, the ridge overlooking Fhionn Lochain can be very exposed in high winds. The climb up to the ridge can be done more gradually if you follow a clockwise circuit. You must take care, however, on the steep paths that descend Meall Biorach.

Walk along a deerstalkers' path that briefly follows the north shore of the lochan before climbing to a bealach or pass between Meall Bhig and the ridge. At the pass, join a path on the right that follows the broad shoulder that leads to the ridge.

Overlooking Fhionn Lochain from the ridge

Higher up, the shoulder flattens off, then boulder fields have to be crossed before the main ridge is reached. A path leads round the top of the coire to Meall Biorach with its summit cairn at 551 metres. From this vantage point, a single sweep of the eye takes in Fhionn Lochain nestling in its 'cauldron', Kintyre across the water and the hills of Jura on the western skyline.

The descent is made by obvious paths from Meall Biorach's summit cairn. It is worth repeating that the descent is best taken slow and steady, because the paths are steep in places. At the base of the hill, rejoin the track for the return to Mid Thundergay.

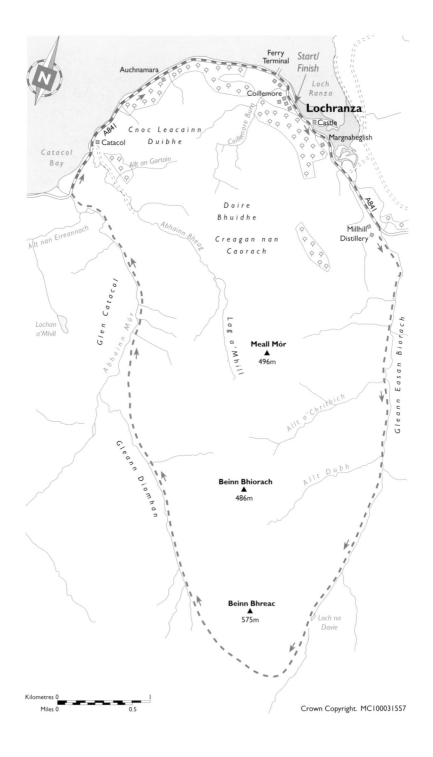

NORTH ARRAN GLENS

This justly popular walk leads deep into mountain country in the north of Arran, without the worry of long, steep gradients or rocky scrambles.

The walk begins in the attractive village of Lochranza, the main settlement in the north of Arran. The village has a dramatic setting. Surrounded by hills, it sits on the shore of its eponymous loch. And jutting into that loch is a narrow neck of land on which sits Lochranza Castle. This gaunt shell is thought to have been built in the 16th century and originally to have been a hunting lodge of the Stewart kings. James IV used the castle to attack the power of the Macdonald Lords of the Isles.

Set off for the southern end of Lochranza, walking past the Isle of Arran Distillery. Arran was famed for its *uisge-beatha*, but the island did not produce single malt whisky for 150 years until the new distillery, with its visitor centre, opened in 1995. Just past the distillery and before a humpback bridge, follow a track to the right. Signposts indicate Gleann Easan Biorach and Loch na Davie.

The track rises to a cleft between the rocky dome of Torr Nead an Eoin on the left and the slopes of Creag a' Chaise on the right. The track crosses a slope overlooking small waterfalls and pools along

INFORMATION

Distance: 17.25km (10.75 miles) circular.

Start and finish: Lochranza village.

Terrain: Good mountain tracks and often very boggy moorland. Final stretch along coast road from Catacol to Lochranza. Map (OS Landranger 69 or Harvey's Arran) and compass essential in glens. Water-resistant footwear recommended.

Public Transport: Western Buses and Royal Mail post buses provide scheduled services to and from Brodick and other coastal communities.

Refreshments: Hotels at Catacol and Lochranza. Isle of Arran Distillery, Lochranza, has a visitor centre with restaurant.

Opening hours: Isle of Arran Distillery, daily 1000-1600 Apr-Oct; for winter hours phone 01770 830264

Arran Distillery, near the start of the walk

the burn that flows out of Loch na Davie, a feature of this walk. Gleann Easan Biorach soon broadens out and the gradient eases, but the track frequently crosses streams and switches repeatedly from firm to boggy going. Remember to look well ahead to plot a course through drier ground.

Higher up the glen, the track fords the Allt Dubh burn at a particularly attractive spot, sheltered by birch trees. Higher still, the burn spills over attractive rock slabs.

Continue on to Loch na Davie, on the watershed between Gleann Easan Biorach and Glen Iorsa to the south. Beyond the loch, the jagged peaks of A'Chir, Beinn Tarsuinn and Beinn Nuis start to appear on the skyline. Don't just look ahead, however, for a golden eagle may be floating high above. One clue to the eagle's presence may be an eerie whoosh of wind through its wings.

(top) Looking back up Gleann Diomhan
(bottom) Waterfall in Gleann Diomhan

Beyond Loch na Davie, the track begins to curve round the base of Beinn Bhreac up to the right. You now approach the halfway point of this glens walk, and fittingly, Cir Mhor appears like an arrow-head to the southeast. The track continues to curve round below Beinn Bhreac, passes a cairn and then climbs up to the bealach or pass leading down to the next glen, Gleann Diomhan.

Follow a track into Gleann Diomhan, keeping a burn to your left. Further down the glen you may hear rushing water in the burn below. The sound comes from an attractive waterfall which can be reached by a careful clamber down a heathery slope. This is a lovely spot for lunch. Although the water falls only some 7 metres, it does so with considerable force into a rock pool.

Continue down the bouldery track to an area enclosed by deer fencing. This is Gleann Diomhan National Nature Reserve, where two endangered varieties of sorbus, or whitebeam, grow. These trees —the Arran whitebeam and Arran Service Tree— are unique to Arran. To view the trees, climb over the deer fence by a ladder stile and follow a track down to a narrow gorge where the trees cling to its rocky walls.

In the 1860s, local people could have done with their own protection from deer. Instead they were turned out of Glen Catacol by the landowner, the 11th Duke of Hamilton, so that he could make money from stalking.

Back on the track, continue down Gleann Diomhan. The track becomes less bouldery after the junction with the track into neighbouring Glen Catacol. Soon you will see house roofs down at Catacol on the coast road. The track clings closer to the burn as it nears Catacol, then passes fields before a fence is crossed by a stile. Head for a clump of trees beside a bridge carrying the coast road over the burn.

The Twelve Apostles at Catacol

Turn right and walk along the road to Catacol, with its hotel and famous 'Twelve Apostles'. This row of 12 cottages was built to house people cleared off the glen. A further 2km of walking along the scenic coastal road takes you past the Lochranza ferry terminal, for Claonaig on Kintyre, then back into the village itself.

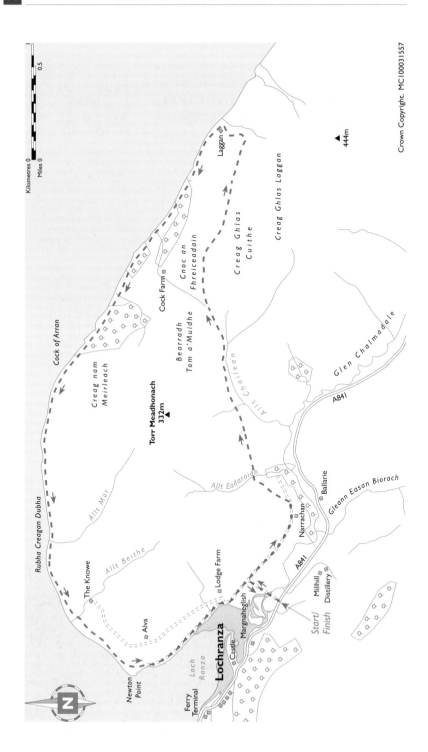

Kilometres 0 0.5 1
Miles 0

Crown Copyright. MC100031557

Cock of Arran

Creag nam Meirleach

Cock Farm

Cnoc an Fhreiceadain

Bearradh Tom a'Muidhe

Creag Ghlas Cuithe

Creag Ghlas Laggan

Laggan

▲ 444m

Torr Meadhonach 332m ▲

Rubha Creagan Dubha

Allt Mór

Allt a' Chailean

Glen Chalmadale

A841

Allt Eadaraigh

The Knowe

Allt Beithe

Lodge Farm

Alva

Newton Point

Loch Ranza

Lochranza

Castle

Margnaheglish

Ferry Terminal

Narrachan

Ballarie

Gleann Easan Biorach

A841

Millhill

Distillery

Start/ Finish

N

THE COCK OF ARRAN

A ruined croft on a hillside. A peculiar rock formation by a seashore. The first was the birthplace of the Macmillan dynasty that produced a major publishing house and a Prime Minister. The second saw a ground-breaking geological discovery that confounded the fundamentalist Christian view that the world was formed during a brief period called the Creation. The ruined croft and the rock formation add special interest to this walk. But even if they did not exist, the Cock of Arran would still be one of Scotland's classic excursions.

The route follows the rugged coastline round the northern tip of Arran. The walk begins at the south end of Lochranza village, beside St Bride's Parish Church. From the church, head a few yards south along the A841 coast road, then cross over and walk down a lane signposted to the Cock of Arran.

Follow the lane past the golf course, then turn right onto a road that gradually gains height, passing cottages on the way. Higher up, join a track signposted to the Cock and Laggan. Cross an old wooden footbridge over a burn and then start the long but gradual climb to the highest point of the walk.

INFORMATION

Distance: 12.25km (7.5 miles) circular.

Start and finish: Lochranza village.

Terrain: Water-resistant footwear needed for several very boggy stretches of hill track. Mainly good track along shoreline. However, awkward scrambling over fallen boulders after Cock is **not recommended for young children**.

Public Transport: Western Buses and Royal Mail post buses provide scheduled services between Brodick and other coastal communities. There is also a car ferry service to Lochranza from Claonaig in Kintyre.

Refreshments: Hotels at Catacol and Lochranza. Isle of Arran Distillery, Lochranza, has visitors' centre with restaurant.

Lochranza Castle, ruined but still impressive

Much of the way uphill is boggy after rain and the track often splits into braids. Look well ahead to pick a way through the wet ground, but also pause to enjoy the unfolding view. Down below, the A841 road heads south past the Isle of Arran Distillery towards Brodick. In the distance, Goatfell and its neighbouring mountains crowd the skyline.

At the top of the slope is another outstanding view, this time over to the island of Bute, the Cowal Peninsula and the mainland. Off the track, downhill among the bracken, stand the remains of Cock Farm. In 1735 this was the birthplace of Malcolm Macmillan, grandfather of Daniel and Alexander Macmillan who founded the famous publishing company, and great-great-grandfather of Harold Macmillan, the Conservative Prime Minister from 1957–63.

Millstone beside old salt pans

Walk down the grassy track to the pretty, white-washed cottage at Laggan. From the cottage, the track heads north through a gap in rocks. It then runs close to the shore where an old mill-wheel rests in the bracken. In this area a slim seam of coal was mined, then burned to boil up seawater in salt pans. The resulting salt was used to cure fish.

The track goes across some boggy and rocky ground, passes through a gap in a stone wall then continues across the grassy foreshore. Ahead, the shore is paved in weirdly shaped red sandstone. Nearby, igneous dykes point north to the cliffs pressing down on the shore.

Sheets of red sandstone roll out to meet the sea

The track goes past the famous Cock of Arran, a large sandstone block that has lost its head since the days that it looked like a cockerel to passing sailors. The way becomes more challenging at the foot of the cliffs. The route wends its way around and over fallen boulders made of very rough conglomerate. Care should be taken here and this section may be too difficult for young children to scramble over.

Eventually you drop down to a shingle shore, and then soon see the first cottages on the approach to Lochranza. The last important landmark on the way to the village is Hutton's Unconformity.

James Hutton has been called the founder of modern geology. He was born in Edinburgh, in 1726, when it was generally believed that the Earth was only 6,000 years old. By the time of his death in 1797, however, he had shown that the Earth's age numbered millions of years.

Hutton travelled throughout Britain and the Continent to study rock formations, and he made a significant breakthrough on Arran. He discovered his 'Unconformity', an unusual rock formation composed of 600-million-year-old schist overlain by 400-million-year-old red sandstone. This proved Hutton's theory that layers of rock could become worn down then covered with fresh rock layers. The Unconformity is on the shore at map reference NR934518.

More interested in grass than golf, a deer trims the rough at Lochranza

On Arran, Hutton also found evidence that helped prove his theory that igneous rocks were produced when magma, or molten rock, was pushed into fissures between solid rock, then cooled in the form of dykes like those on this route.

The walk continues along one of Arran's raised shorelines, turning the corner into Loch Ranza. Raised shorelines were created when land, compressed by glaciers, rose again after the end of the ice age.

Looking down the valley towards Lochranza

The track passes the first cottages then swings round to the north shore of Loch Ranza. Now on the final leg, join the tarmac road at a row of houses and continue on to rejoin the lane that runs by the golf course. Before leaving the area you might like to visit the dramatic ruin of Lochranza Castle, the earliest parts of which date back to the 14th century.

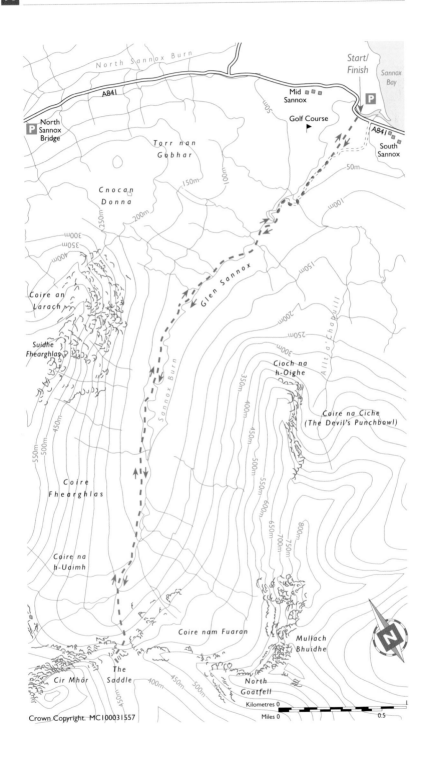

GLEN SANNOX

Glen Sannox is one of the chief delights of Arran. This beautiful glen offers tranquil spots for riverside picnics or access to the wild heart of Arran, the mountains in the island's north-east corner.

This walk follows a track through the glen. It ends at a rock staircase below a difficult scramble to the Saddle, the pass between the steep slopes of North Goatfell and Cir Mhor.

For most of the way, the climb is very gradual, but the track often disappears into boggy ground. The walk starts opposite a telephone box and car park beside Sannox Bay, just south of the golf course. Cross the road to a lane beside a white cottage. Here, a sign points to the glen. Some yards on is the old graveyard where the body of Edwin Rose, victim of the famous 'Arran Murder', is interred.

In 1889, Rose, a London builder's clerk, visited Scotland for his summer holiday. He befriended John Watson Laurie, a patternmaker at the Springburn locomotive works in Glasgow, and they travelled to Arran. One afternoon, the pair set off to climb

With Cir Mhor in the distance, the track cuts through purple heather to the head of the glen

Old graveyard at Glen Sannox

Goatfell. That evening, a lone and exhausted Laurie was seen coming out of Glen Sannox and passing the graveyard.

Several days passed before Rose was posted missing. Some 200 people scoured the mountainsides. Finally, a local fisherman noticed 'an offensive odour' near some boulders in Coire nam Fuaran, overlooking upper Glen Sannox. Pulling aside the rocks, the fisherman found Rose, his pockets empty and his face 'fearfully and terribly smashed'. When Laurie was caught, he admitted stealing Rose's luggage from their lodgings, but denied murder. Nevertheless he was convicted, narrowly avoided execution, and died 41 years later in a criminal asylum.

On which cheerful thought, continue down the lane flanked by ferns and rowan trees. Soon you cross a stile beside a sign that requests that dogs be kept on leads because of grazing sheep.

An unmetalled track leads on to a shallow stream, easily crossed. Ahead, a brick hut marks the site where in 1839 mining began for barytes, a material used in paint manufacturing. Here, around 10 men were employed, while back on the shore, others made barrels to send the barytes to the mainland. Veer left before the hut and arrive at Sannox Burn. Wooden piles are all that remain of a footbridge, so the burn has to be crossed by stepping stones.

Beyond the burn, the flanks of the U-shaped, glacier-gouged glen start to close in. Up to the left, the rocks on Cioch na h-Oighe glint in the sun. On the right, the steep slopes of Suidhe Fhearghas also rise up, covered in heather and polished rock slabs. And ahead in the distance is the arrowhead outline of Cir Mhor, a constant companion on this journey. Though only 799m high, Cir Mhor presents a very rugged challenge, even to the experienced hillwalker.

The track follows the north bank of the burn, sometimes crossing streams. Go quietly, and you may see a lizard scuttling across the track. Further up the glen, the track often splits into braids that may run into bog. It pays to keep your head up while bogtrotting so that drier routes can be found.

Much of the track, nevertheless, has been considerably improved. In the late 1990s, stone paving and culverts were laid on the track leading up to the Saddle and down into neighbouring Glen Rosa. Scottish Natural Heritage estimate that the amount spent on Glen Sannox alone was £155,000.

Sannox Burn, with the rock slabs of Cioch na h-Oighe glinting in the sun

In the upper half of the glen, pause by the Sannox Burn where the water skims over beautiful rock shelves. Continue past banks of waist-high heather and follow the track up to the head of the glen.

The walk assumes a more serious mood where the track crosses the Sannox Burn for the last time. The track starts to rise steeply up a paved staircase towards the cliffs below the Saddle.

The walk ends where the paving finishes. Beyond this, the route clambers over awkward rock shelves then up a steep, slippery and midge-infested rock chimney to the Saddle. Only experienced rock scramblers should attempt to reach the Saddle.

Before heading back through the glen, look round at the impressive cliffs and corries—possibly the last things that Edwin Rose ever saw.

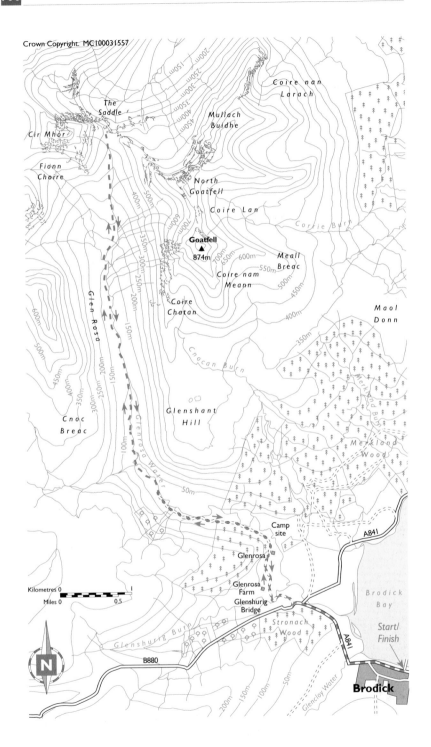

Crown Copyright. MC100031557

GLEN ROSA

Glen Rosa has given many visitors their first taste of Arran mountain country. There could hardly be a better introduction. The entrance to Glen Rosa lies only a short distance from Brodick, but more than that, the glen offers a steady and not too arduous climb through beautiful scenery.

Even the sound Glen Rosa implies beauty, but the name apparently means horse-river valley. Never mind, that distinguished 19th-century judge and traveller, Lord Cockburn, pronounced his verdict on 'Glenrosie' as a 'valley well worth spending a day in'. He recorded in his circuit journeys diary: 'All gushing with the dearest water tumbling over granite; deep sides, browned with chocolate-covered autumn fern, many dark rocky peaks, and the upper end enclosed by as striking an assemblage of black and precipitous mountain-tops as is often to be seen.'

That description still stands today, though 'dark rocky peaks' suggests a forbidding place, when in fact the upper end of the glen is less hemmed-in than that of its neighbour, Glen Sannox.

INFORMATION

Distance: 18.5km (11.5miles).

Start and finish: Ferry terminal, Brodick.

Terrain: Tarmac pavements and roads between ferry terminal and Glen Rosa campsite, then mountain track to the Saddle. Walking boots recommended.

Public Transport: At Brodick, bus to junction with B880 String Road can save time.

Refreshments: Wide variety of pubs and cafes in Brodick area.

Broad track entering Glen Rosa

Day visitors from the mainland will save valuable time by taking a bus from the ferry terminal to travel the 2km north along the A841 coast road to the junction with the B880 String Road. This may seem a small saving, but walkers have often missed the last ferry home by underestimating the return journey between Brodick and the Saddle at the head of Glen Rosa.

Classic view up Glen Rosa to Cir Mhor

Walkers who get off the bus at the junction should walk along the String Road for a short distance then turn right up a minor road, signposted 'Cart Track and Glen Rosa 1 Mile'. The minor road passes houses and ends near the Glen Rosa campsite, in an attractive grassy spot beside Glenrosa Water. The route now joins a rough cart track that continues the way through pleasant, 'softer' scenery before entering the glen itself.

The track turns northward, passing moraines—mounds of boulders and gravel left by retreating glaciers. Further on, a bridge crosses over the Garbh Allt burn where it tumbles down through large boulders to join Glenrosa Water. Glen Rosa can now been seen ahead, its U-shaped form another product of the gouging forces of the Ice Age.

Pyramid-shaped Cir Mhor stands at the head of the glen. Framed by the slopes of Goatfell on the right and Beinn Tarsuinn on the left, Cir Mhor provides one of the classic views on Arran.

The track soon passes a sign for the National Trust for Scotland which has Goatfell and the surrounding mountains and glens in its care. An example of NTS environmental work can be seen further up the glen where an area of ground has been fenced off from deer and sheep to allow natural woodland to regenerate.

This 'Glen Rosa Exclosure' was supported by the Heritage Lottery Fund and also involves the Forestry Commission. The track passes through the exclosure by gates and continues up the glen close to Glenrosa Water. This lovely burn flows and tumbles down the glen, its clear water revealing stones and gravel at the bottom of its pools. The track allows good going up the glen, thanks to considerable path-renewal work carried out in recent years. At a fork, keep right, crossing a burn to continue into the upper glen.

Towards the Saddle, the pass or bealach at the head of the glen, the track passes huge boulders, more debris of the Ice Age. The track steepens on the final stretch to the stone slabs of the Saddle at about 460m. Cir Mhor rears up dramatically on the left while a ridge on the right rises more gradually towards North Goatfell.

Looking over to the Witch's Step from the Saddle

Best view of all, maybe, is northwards to the rugged northern wall of neighbouring Glen Sannox, and the famous gap called the Witch's Step. The panorama from the Saddle confirms the fact that Arran's mountains make up in grandeur for what they may lack in stature compared to other hills.

Hillwalkers frequently continue their journey by descending from the Saddle into Glen Sannox. The steepness and awkwardness of that section of route puts it out of the scope of this book.

The return walk, of course, gives a different perspective and a chance to enjoy views up to the right of the steep slopes of A'Chir and Beinn Tarsuinn. The section from the String Road to Brodick should be done on foot if possible because it passes Arran Heritage Museum, with its smiddy, shop and tearoom.

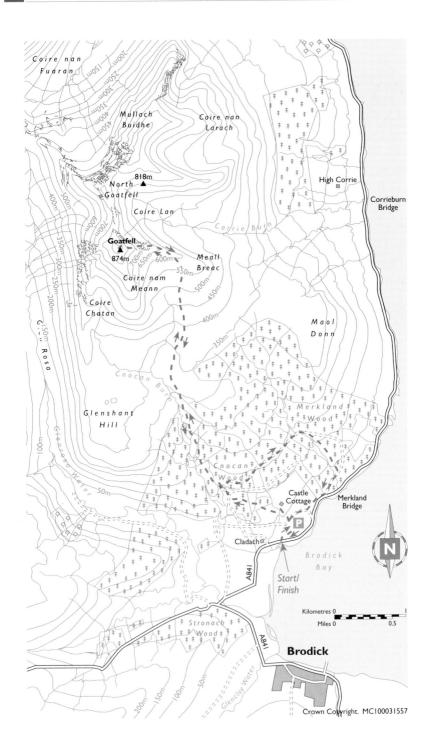

BRODICK CASTLE AND GOATFELL

As the CalMac ferry *Caledonian Isles* approaches Brodick pier, two things draw the visitor's eye: the red sandstone form of Brodick Castle standing among the trees that line the north side of Brodick Bay, and the grey boulder-strewn bulk of Goatfell that dominates the whole island of Arran. Both castle or mountain would make an ideal day out on their own. This walk brings them together.

Walkers making solely for Goatfell generally set off from the car park at Claddach, a short distance west of the pedestrian entrance to Brodick Castle garden and country park where this walk begins.

Entry to the grounds involves a moderate charge (£3.50 per adult in 2004, National Trust for Scotland members free). From the pedestrian entrance, walk up a track through trees. Soon, the castle appears high up on the left, its Saltire flapping proudly from its main tower. Take the steps up to the castle. The oldest part of Brodick Castle, the east tower, is believed to date from the 1500s. Around that period it is thought to have been attacked and demolished twice.

The castle, seat of the powerful Dukes of Hamilton for several centuries, was extended considerably in the 1800s. When the 12th Duke died in 1895, his daughter married the Duke of Montrose. The castle was handed over to the NTS in 1958, and the

INFORMATION

Distance: 13.75km (8.5miles) circular.

Start and finish: Pedestrian entrance to Brodick Castle.

Terrain: Good woodland paths through Brodick Castle country park. Mountain track on Goatfell is well paved on lower stretch, but very rough and steep on ridge to summit. **Hillwalking boots and knowledge of map and compass essential.**

Public transport: On Arran, Western Buses meet the ferry to take passengers to Brodick Castle and other destinations around the island.

Refreshments: Shop and cafe at castle. Wide choice of pubs and cafes in Brodick.

Opening hours: Brodick Castle: Easter to end Oct, daily 1100-1630. Country Park open all year

Brodick Castle

Goatfell, with Brodick Castle peeping through the trees near the shore

public can now tour the rooms which contain outstanding items of silverware, porcelain and paintings.

At the top of the steps, turn right and walk down a path that leads through a gate that exits the castle garden. You can continue downhill to visit the reception centre, but on this occasion turn left and follow signs for Goatfell. Cross the main driveway, and take the path waymarked to the Countryside Centre and Ranger Services.

Go through the Countryside Centre courtyard and join a woodland path waymarked for Goatfell and the Hamilton Cemetery. In the attractive wood, which has tall Scots pine and native Arran whitebeam, cross a small gorge by footbridges. Further on you encounter the remains of rhododendrons that have been cut back to clear the area of this picturesque pest. Only a few years after this operation, rhodies were starting to grow back.

The path continues to the walled cemetery containing the graves of several members of the Hamilton dynasty. A short distance beyond the cemetery the path joins a broad track. Turn right and head uphill, following red and blue marker signs.

Track leading to Goatfell in the distance

About 200 metres on, the blue trail branches right. Continue on the red trail, signposted to Goatfell, until this trail, in turn, branches right into a plantation. This is the branch you will take on the return from Goatfell. Continue uphill and follow a narrow mountain track past a Goatfell sign. The track rises through bracken, heather and silver birch, eventually arriving at a small burn bridged by railway sleepers. This is a pleasant place to pause and admire the view down to Brodick Bay.

A short distance above the burn, go through a gate in a deer fence. Continue up the steep track and come over a rise that gives a clear view of Goatfell and the route up to the 874-metre summit.

The summit track follows a series of cairns towards the ridge on the northern skyline. On a fine day, there should be no problem about routefinding because the track is clearly visible and well paved, and there will probably be other walkers using it. Nevertheless, this is real mountain country, a place where map and compass knowledge is essential. The ridge rises steeply, and just below the summit, detours will have to be made round large boulders.

The view from the summit is unforgettable. Close to are Cir Mhor and other jagged neighbouring peaks, and Glen Sannox can be seen below, just to the north. The view extends over Arran and across the Firth of Clyde to the mainland.

Walkers rest on the summit of Goatfell

After a well-earned lunch, the temptation is to make for North Goatfell and follow the ridge down to the Saddle for a return leg down Glen Rosa. This should not be contemplated by inexperienced walkers, because rotten granite on the ridge gives a treacherous footing.

Instead, retrace your steps carefully down the mountain until you eventually arrive back at the

Heading back down the mountain towards Brodick Bay

branch mentioned earlier for the red trail. Turn left into this branch, the Merkland Gorge Trail, and continue through woodland and a grassy avenue until you cross the Merkland Burn by a bridge or stepping stones. Beyond the bridge, turn downhill, following a path by the Merkland Burn. This stretch of the walk goes through lovely woodland containing Douglas fir and oak, and the burn drops down through a series of small falls.

Brodick Castle

When the path reaches a forestry road, turn right and cross Merkland Burn by another bridge. Just before the road reaches the main coast road, turn right along a path that skirts parkland and meets the driveway that leads up to Brodick Castle.